PENGUIN BUSINESS
MULTIBAGGER STOCKS

Prasenjit Paul is the author of the Amazon-bestselling book *How to Avoid Loss and Earn Consistently in the Stock Market*. He has been investing in the stock market since 2010 and has a history of identifying several multibagger stocks, such as Chemcrux Enterprises, Lancer Container, Sirca Paints, Caplin Point Lab and Can Fin Homes. In the process, he has multiplied his portfolio by more than 100 times in the last decade. To spread financial literacy, he maintains a presence across various social media platforms, such as YouTube, Twitter, Telegram and Facebook.

Follow Prasenjit Paul at:

www.prasenjitpaul.com

▶ @PKPaul or @PKPaulBengali

🐦 PaulAsset

✈ PrasenjitPaulVerified

f PrasenjitPaulOfficial

📷 PrasenjitPaulOfficial

MULTIBAGGER STOCKS

HOW TO MULTIPLY WEALTH IN THE SHARE MARKET

PRASENJIT PAUL

PENGUIN
BUSINESS

An imprint of Penguin Random House

PENGUIN BUSINESS

USA | Canada | UK | Ireland | Australia
New Zealand | India | South Africa | China | Singapore

Penguin Business is part of the Penguin Random House group of companies
whose addresses can be found at global.penguinrandomhouse.com

Published by Penguin Random House India Pvt. Ltd
4th Floor, Capital Tower 1, MG Road,
Gurugram 122 002, Haryana, India

First published in Penguin Business by Penguin Random House India 2023

10 9 8 7 6 5 4 3 2

ISBN 9780143456476

Typeset in Adobe Caslon Pro by MAP Systems, Bengaluru, India
Printed at Repro India Limited

www.penguin.co.in

Contents

My Personal Investments That Generated Multifold Returns

Stock Name	Holding Period	Return on Investment
Chemcrux Enterprise	2017 onwards	40 times and counting
Lancer Container	2017 to 2021	9 times
Sirca Paints	2018 to 2021	3 times
Gujarat Themis Biosyn	2020 onwards	7 times and counting
Can Fin Homes	2013 to 2018	16 times
Caplin Point Lab	2014 to 2016	13 times
Sanwaria Consumers	2017 to 2018	3 times
Ajanta Pharma	2012 to 2015	15 times
Atul Auto	2013 to 2014	3 times
Suprajit Engineering	2014 to 2016	3 times

Refer **Important Points to Note** on the following page.

My other multibagger stocks include SNL Bearings, Shree Pushkar Chemicals, Future Enterprises Limited, Bajaj Healthcare, SKP Bearings, Bombay Metrics Supply Chain, Mayur Uniquoters, PI Industries, Avanti Feeds, Torrent Pharma, etc.

Important Points to Note:

1. My investment in Chemcrux Enterprises and Lancer Container can be verified from the official BSE India website as I held more than 1 per cent of the company's stock. One can also visit https://www.screener.in/people/ (paid feature) and search with my name 'Prasenjit Kumar Paul' for a detailed, consolidated view.

2. The number of wealth destroyers in my investment career is probably higher than the number of multibaggers. I lost money on stocks like MRSS, Focus Suites, Sarveshwar Foods, Global Education, Jhandewalas Foods, Sysco Industries, Shanti Overseas, Mandhana Industries, Sintex Industries and many more. Interestingly, despite these losers, my overall portfolio multiplied by more than 100 times in value over the last decade.

Why This Book?

The term 'multibagger stock', coined by the legendary investor Peter Lynch, refers to a stock that generates multiple times' returns on investment. A stock that generates 100 per cent returns is called a 'two-bagger'; one that generates a tenfold return on investment is called a 'ten-bagger' and so on. Any stock that generates manifold returns from the investment value can be called a multibagger. You might often come across media reports that say:

'An investment of Rs 10,000 made in Infosys in 1993 is now worth Rs 4 crore.'

or

'An investment of Rs 1 lakh made in HDFC Bank in 1995 is now worth Rs 8 crore.'

But before getting enthused by such statements, let's understand the three major practical problems associated with them:

Problem 1

For every HDFC Bank or Infosys, there are a few hundred stocks that reduced every investment of Rs 1 lakh in them to zero over long periods. For example, back in the 1980s and 1990s, Hindustan Motors (maker of Ambassador cars) was a blue-chip stock and was part of the Nifty 50 and Sensex. In fact, Hindustan Motors was the single largest car manufacturer in India for decades. To be seen in a white Ambassador car or a yellow Ambassador taxi was once a status symbol. But, if you invested in Hindustan Motors shares in the 1990s, that investment would be worth close to zero today. In recent days too, we have had well-known stocks like Educomp, Unitech, Reliance Capital, Suzlon and Cox & Kings as examples of wealth destroyers. Apart from these famous names, there are hundreds of stocks that have crashed by 90–95 per cent over any four-to-five-year period. Thus, headlines that report Rs 1 lakh in HDFC Bank in 1995 growing to Rs 8 crore today are just one side of the coin and not the complete picture.

Problem 2

Investors who bought shares in HDFC Bank or Infosys in the 1990s most likely sold out their investments in the next market crash or booked profit in the next phase of market euphoria. There were multiple instances when HDFC Bank crashed by 40–60 per cent, a fall significant enough to shake investor confidence. Do you know of any investor who kept those shares over a long period of twenty or twenty-five years? If you do, then you can stop reading this book and learn from that person. Obviously, it shouldn't be a case of someone holding on to shares by default, having purchased a few shares in the 1990s and then, having misplaced or lost the share certificates, was unable to sell them all these years. If you know of any investor who put money into a few select shares that generated more than a thousand-fold return on their investments, then, obviously, that person will be the best teacher to give you a lesson on multibaggers.

Problem 3

Just because HDFC Bank generated returns of 800x in the past twenty-five years, would you invest in the stock now, hoping for returns of another 800x over the next twenty-five years? If yes, then that would be a big mistake. At best, such stocks can compound your wealth at 10–20 per cent annually over the long run but surely can't repeat those extraordinary returns they once generated. Take the example of another well-known stock, ITC, which generated around five times the return on investment over the seven-year period between 2009 and 2015. Back in 2013–15, almost all analysts were bullish on ITC. Media reports highlighted stories of how monthly investments in ITC could create huge wealth over a four-to-five-year period. It appeared as if things were so easy that one could literally multiply one's wealth while doing nothing. From 2014 to 2021, if you had continued your monthly investments in ITC, then you would have ended up with almost zero returns. Despite being one of the finest companies in the country, ITC underperformed for eight long years! Even a no-brainer bank fixed deposit can double your investment in eight to nine years! One can argue that ITC offered generous dividends in those years. The fact is, if you kept that money in your savings bank account, you would have earned that same dividend as interest income without having had to endure the stock market volatility. If your target is to earn savings bank account-like returns from equity investment, then it is better to stay away from the stock market. When there are opportunities for earning tension-free fixed income from bank deposits while doing nothing, then why put up with the volatility and uncertainty of the stock market for modest returns?

> *'If equity investment can't earn at least double the bank fixed deposit over the long run, then it's time to reconsider your investment strategy.'*

The point I want to convey here is that if you find media coverage on how a stock generated ten times or 100 times returns in the past years, then most likely the same stock can't repeat the same performance in the coming years. Excessive optimism over the ITC stock and intense media coverage of it during 2012–15 were among the reasons for its poor performance in subsequent years. ITC can again generate wealth for investors in the absence of excessive optimism over it.

> *'Media coverage on multibaggers with 50–100 times returns ensures that most likely the stock can't repeat the same performance in the coming days.'*

So far, I hope you understand that attention-grabbing headlines like 'Rs 10,000 investment in Infosys is now worth Rs 4 crore' can at best motivate you but surely can't help you to earn multibagger returns from the same stock.

The best guide is always the person who has travelled the path. In the Indian context, veteran investors like Vijay Kedia, Ashish Kacholia, Ramdeo Agarwal, Dolly Khanna, Ashish Chugh, etc., have had a successful track record of discovering multiple multibagger stocks over the last few decades. I would prefer to learn from investors like them, who have travelled the path, rather than from academicians who flaunt their theoretical knowledge. The problem is that none of these successful investors has written their principles of investing in a book. This book is meant to fill that void. Unlike those veterans, I don't have decades of investing experience. However, my active involvement in the stock market since 2010, witnessing multiple bull–bear cycles and discovering multiple multibagger stocks in the process, gives me the confidence to write this book, which should surely help a lot of investors. In fact, if properly utilized, this book, costing a few hundred rupees, can build a foundation for you to be able to earn many crores of rupees over the long run.

The first part of the book covers my investment journey, my initial struggles, the books that helped me a lot, how I evolved as an investor and my journey with multibagger stocks. After that, you will learn about the driving forces behind any multibagger stock. There might be some irrationality in their short-term price movement. However, long-term stock price movement is always backed by multiple logical factors. You will know the triggers behind multibagger returns as well as the factors behind wealth destruction. The book also explores an important aspect of when to average (buy more) and when to sell. If the price of a stock moves up just after you have bought it, you will regret not having bought more of it. If it goes down, then you will regret having bought it at a higher price. And if the price remains static over years, you will regret not having done proper analysis! So, regret is a constant in your investment journey! This is the reason it is your post-purchase actions—more than stock selection—that will decide your wealth-creation journey.

Proper allocation makes a lot of difference, of course.

When a stock with a 2 per cent portfolio allocation generates twenty times the returns, it won't make any difference. However, if the same stock has a 15 per cent initial allocation, then the entire portfolio turns multibagger.'

Finally, the book covers important 'Dos and Don'ts'. In your quest for multibagger stocks, you shouldn't fall for 'multi-beggars', i.e., stocks that destroy wealth. More than multibagger stock selection, successful wealth creation requires the avoidance of wealth destroyers so that your overall investment portfolio can multiply.

> *'More than multibagger stock selection, the target is to build a multibagger portfolio that can multiply your wealth over the long run.'*

Considering our current fast-paced lifestyle, I maintained the 'keep it short and simple' (KISS) approach while writing this book. My objective is to be to the point and to write in very simple English, so that no reader gets bored with it. I remember purchasing an international bestseller once with a lot of enthusiasm. It was a self-help book from Amazon. When the book was delivered, I discovered that it had 800 pages. The size of the book and the small font size of the print simply killed my enthusiasm for it. I wasn't able to finish the book but opted for a book-summarizing paid subscription service to grab the principles communicated in the book. This book is for the masses; anyone with a basic knowledge of the stock market can easily understand the principles mentioned in this book. That is why I have tried to ensure that the pages are kept to the minimum possible and that the book uses a medium-sized font. I can easily stretch the number of pages simply by inserting quotations by famous investors, lengthy references and whatnot, but then the book will lose its appeal to the mass audience.

> *'The objective of this book is to reach a mass audience with to-the-point writing, in short and simple English, so that even a new investor with a basic understanding of the stock market can grab the ideas communicated in the book.'*

If you have never invested in the stock market or are a complete amateur, then you should first read my bestseller *How to Avoid Loss and Earn Consistently in the Stock Market*, to be able to better understand this one.

Now, ask yourself:

- Are you looking to multiply your investments over the long term?
- Do you want to explore the driving forces behind multibagger stocks?
- Do you want to learn from a person who has done the multibagger journey?
- Are you looking for a short, simple and to-the-point guide in simple English for your financial well-being?

If your answer to any of the above is 'yes', then you are at the right place. You have already taken the first step by purchasing this book. If you can utilize the book properly, I am sure the few hundred rupees of investment in the book will become the most productive multibagger in your life!

Chapter 1

My Journey with Multibaggers

1.1 Introduction

This is not a typical theoretical book, but rather a practical, easy-to-follow guide. This book is all about my successful journey in the stock market and what I have learnt from it. I strongly believe that as I have already travelled the path, I can be a proper guide for you in your multibagger hunt. This chapter is all about my journey and insights from it.

I was not born with a golden spoon in my mouth; nor did I inherit any wealth to start equity investing with. My wealth is entirely self-acquired. Like many of you, I am from a middle-class Indian family that prioritizes job safety above business and the stock market. Thus, I strongly believe that if I can succeed in the stock market, then you too can.

1.2 My Journey

Here is my journey in three phases.

Phase 1, 2010–2013

I started my investment journey in 2010 while I was still a college student. You might be surprised to know that I had no background in the subject of commerce. I was a higher secondary-level (10+2, as they refer to it) science student who then opted to do his bachelor's in engineering, in information technology from Bengal Engineering and Science University, Shibpur (currently known as Indian Institute of Engineering Science and Technology). Before my admission to the course, I had no idea what information technology (IT) was all about. I opted for it just because everyone else was optimistic about it, and spoke of its bright prospects and how one could easily get a job after studying the subject. It was during my college years that I read the bestselling book *Rich Dad Poor Dad* by Robert T. Kiyosaki, which changed my life forever. After reading that book, I was determined not to do a job but to become an entrepreneur. I was involved in two start-ups with my college friends, but both failed. During my college years, my father suggested that instead of keeping all my savings in the bank, I could invest a part of it in the stock market. Since my higher secondary days, I used to earn a few thousand rupees by giving private tuitions to other students. Those few thousands constituted my initial capital. There was no capital that came from any external sources. The biggest barrier for me was the lack of learning resources. Today, there are hundreds of free videos and 'how-to' guides on investment that can help an amateur learn the basics of stock market investing within a few days from the comfort of his or her home. Nowadays, opening a trading account is just a matter of a few clicks. But in those days, high-speed Internet was a distant dream, and there were certainly no YouTube videos from which to learn even the basics of investing. I was clueless about how to even place buy or sell orders online. My father used to call his broker for trade placement and had never done online trading. For me, it was difficult to call the broker during college hours, so I really needed an online solution. Remember, those were the days of 2G mobile phones. Android still hadn't made inroads into the telecom world, and no brokerage firm had an online mobile application for trading. They only had web-based applications. After college hours, I used to travel to my broker's office by public transport to learn the basics, such as placing online buy/sell orders and other stuff. New-age tech trading platforms like Groww, Paytm Money, etc., didn't exist, and companies like Zerodha and Upstox had just started their journey. Even Zerodha had a bulky web-based trading application borrowed from the NSE. So the learning curve was steep. The only saving grace was the free Wi-Fi in our college hostel, which helped me discover many great investment books. I was able to read insightful content and also track the daily market. I am sure that without the hostel Wi-Fi, I would never have succeeded in the stock market. Instead of sitting here and writing this book, I would probably have been in some multinational company.

Just like every other beginner who started his or her investment journey as a teenager, I faced two major hurdles:

1. Lack of sufficient funds
2. Lack of mentorship and handholding during the initial days

I believe these two challenges are actually blessings in disguise. You are bound to lose money to some extent in the initial stages of your investment journey. If you start with a few thousand and lose 40–50 per cent of it, the absolute loss still remains insignificant and you can quickly bounce back. However, if you start with Rs 10 lakh and lose half of it, then it would be a big blow to your morale. Often, investors have left the stock market after such a major loss. Thus, it actually helps to start small. Insufficient funds mean you need to carefully spend on learning resources. You can't afford high-value courses, mentorship programmes, etc. Quality books are the cheapest and best resource to learn from. To save some money, I used to purchase second-hand books from the College Street and Park Street areas in Kolkata. That investment of a few hundred rupees in books built the foundation for my earning crores in later years. I still have those second-hand books—*One Up on Wall Street*, *The Intelligent Investor*, the Rich Dad Poor Dad series, *The Five Rules for Successful Stock Investing* and many others—that shaped my future. During this period, stocks like Ajanta Pharma, Atul Auto, PI Industries, Mayur Uniquoters, etc., multiplied my initial investments. Obviously, there were a lot of instances where I lost money while experimenting with various investment techniques. I consider all such losses as tuition fees. During one summer vacation, I started trading intraday. After thirty days of it, I realized that this was not worth dedicating time and energy to. Day trading is the most mentally exhausting and intensely engaging process in the stock market. Success is not possible in day trading if you are in a full-time job.

After completing my bachelor's degree in 2013, I had job offers from TCS and IBM. My parents always dreamt about their son working in a multinational company. After all, that is considered a status symbol in Indian social circles. However, I was so inspired by the book *Rich Dad Poor Dad* that, since day one of reading it, I was determined not to do any job to avoid the rat race that is corporate employment. It was a nightmare for me to tell my parents that I would not do a job but would focus full-time on the stock market. My father was a retired bank employee and my mother a homemaker, so it was very hard for them to digest this. Although it was my father who had introduced me to the stock market, he never dreamt that his son would take it so seriously! Having been a bank employee, he was of the view that one's primary source of income must be a stable and secure job, and that part of one's savings could be channelled into the stock market. Thus, there was immense resistance to my adventurous approach of not doing a job but focusing on the stock market as a full-time means of earning. To make it worse, the stock market witnessed a dull phase between 2011 and 2013. I had no steady source of income and no proven track record of earning significantly from stocks. It was indeed a very bold decision on my part, because if the dull market phase had continued for another few years, then I might have been forced to turn to the corporate world. Fortunately, the stock market revived and witnessed a strong bull run in 2014, and I tasted my first major success.

Phase 2 (2014–2017)

The stock market had witnessed a dull phase between 2011 and 2013. The NIFTY 50, the benchmark index, tanked about 30 per cent in 2011 alone. High inflation, rising interest rates and rupee depreciation dented the prospects of corporate India. Back then, multiple corruption charges against the Manmohan Singh-led UPA government had surfaced too. Prime Minister Singh started losing popularity. Arvind Kejriwal and Anna Hazare had started an anti-corruption movement that had started grabbing headlines. All this political chaos weakened the stock market further.

But after September 2013, when Narendra Modi was announced as the BJP's prime ministerial candidate for the 2014 Lok Sabha elections, the market started showing some signs of strength. The election resulted in a landslide victory for the Narendra Modi-led National Democratic Alliance (NDA), with the BJP emerging as the single largest party, ending twenty-five years of coalition rule at the Centre. From its September 2013 low, the NIFTY 50 rose by around 60 per cent by the end of 2014. At this stage, for the first time, I experienced multibagger gains and my investments grew to a modest sum of Rs 7–8 lakh.

Since 2010, I had been rereading the Rich Dad Poor Dad book series (three in all) many times and was determined to create multiple sources of income for myself. I realized that an external source of income would help a lot in equity investing. The target was to create four or five sources of income to attain financial freedom for myself. So here were my five attempts to accomplish this:

Attempt 1—During my college years, I founded two start-ups with my friends. The first was to create a marketplace for second-hand books, and the second was an edtech platform for competitive exam preparations. After some initial traction, both businesses failed.

Attempt 2—Simultaneously with the start-ups, during my college years, I started my equity investment journey. The target was to create some sort of steady, periodic (monthly or quarterly) income. Although I failed to create steady, periodic income from the stock market, over the long run this exercise made my fortune.

Attempt 3—Realizing that looking at the stock market as a monthly steady income source was not feasible, I started focusing on writing blogs (articles) to share my learnings and experience in the stock market. Back in those days, monetizing blogs via Google AdSense used to fetch an adequate monthly income. Prior to the arrival of Reliance Jio in 2016–17, Internet access was expensive and mass video consumption was a distant dream. So websites with quality text content used to get huge traffic that helped them earn advertising revenue from Google AdSense. My blogs received good feedback from the audience, and the website traffic started increasing. Encouraged by this, I submitted my blog to Google to qualify for advertising income. To my utter disappointment, Google rejected my submission twice, and my dream of creating an excellent passive source of income was shattered.

Attempt 4—Despite Google AdSense having rejected my blog for advertising revenue, my articles started gaining popularity among the audience. I would receive great feedback and compliments, and thus the idea of writing a book came to my mind. Again, the target was to create a passive income source. My first book, *How to Avoid Loss and Earn Consistently in the Stock Market*, was published in 2015 and was an instant hit. Although I didn't spend a single penny to advertise the book, word-of-mouth publicity did wonders for it. Finally, my dream of creating a steady passive source of income succeeded. The monthly cash flow from the sales of the book helped me a lot, especially during the bear market phase, when many stocks are traded cheaply. Since 2015, my earnings from the book were entirely channelled into the stock market.

Attempt 5—While my articles gained in popularity, many readers suggested that I start advisory services, which also clicked well. The income from my advisory services supported all my personal and business expenses while the cash flow from the book helped me develop a strong capital base in the stock market.

Thus, I succeeded in creating two income sources after five attempts, and also compounded my equity investments. By the way, back in 2013–14, the rejection of my blog by Google AdSense for advertising income had been one of my biggest disappointments. Many years later, as Internet access became cheaper and faster, and YouTube videos gained popularity, I renewed my desire to earn passive income from the Google advertising network. I started making YouTube videos in late 2020 on two channels named 'Prasenjit Paul' and the second one 'Prasenjit Paul (Bengali Videos)'. This time I easily succeeded in making passive income, because by then I already had an existing audience base who had liked my book very much and were eager to hear me too. Remember, the first crore is always very difficult, but once you reach that mark then its multiplication becomes a lot easier.

Another insight I would like to share is that the stock market never moves in a linear way, and this must always be kept in mind. A few years of a bull run must be followed by a bear market. There will be times when, regardless of your talent, knowledge and experience, you will lose money, or at best can't make money. During such difficult periods, multiple income sources can rescue you.

'Never hope for periodic (monthly/quarterly) income from the equity market unless you already have a large capital base or existing multiple sources of income.'

After the 2014 bull run, the stock market again entered a dull phase in 2015 and 2016. The infamous demonetization of late 2016 created havoc in the market but made way for the strong bull run of 2017. During this period, my investments in Can Fin Homes, Caplin Point Lab, Avanti Feeds, Suprajit Engineering, Kovai Medical, SNL Bearings and Sanwaria Consumers, among some other stocks, helped my overall portfolio to multiply by ten-to-twelve times. In the latter part of this book, you will find case studies and learnings from my investment, along with the secrets of multibaggers.

Phase 3 (2017–2022)

By the end of 2017, I had a very comfortable capital base and my confidence was running high from the success of my many multibagger picks—and that's when I made a few mistakes. My first costly mistake was to take a loan to buy an office and a Mercedes car. I had enough capital to fund both purchases. However, I thought that I could easily grow my investments at 30–40 per cent annually while continuing to paying only 7–8 per cent interest on the loan. The idea was that borrowed funds would help me multiply my wealth as my investments could generate at least double the interest rate at which I had borrowed. This strategy will work fine only as long as the market is in the bull phase. But whenever liquidity dries up, loans paid via equated monthly instalments (EMIs) become a challenge. The NIFTY small-cap index crashed by 40 per cent in 2018 alone. The decline continued until March 2020. From its peak in 2018, the index dropped by more than 60 per cent. To give this perspective, during the 2007–08 market crash, the benchmark NIFTY 50 had declined by around 54 per cent, while during 2018–20 the small-cap index declined more than that. As my portfolio had almost 100 per cent allocation in small-cap stocks, the crash of 2018–20 taught me enough lessons that 2007–08 might have to some other investor of that time.

My second major mistake was that almost 100 per cent of my portfolio consisted of low-volume stocks. With the market decline, liquidity dried up, making it tough to exit from one's positions. Since then, I have changed my allocation strategy. Instead of keeping 100 per cent of investments in low-volume small-cap stocks, I started maintaining a 50:50 allocation of funds in low-volume and high-volume stocks.

Over the 2017–18 period, my investments were concentrated in the following five stocks:

1. KP Energy
2. Chemcrux Enterprises
3. Lancer Container
4. MRSS
5. Focus Suites

Apart from these five stocks, I invested in stocks such as Sirca Paints, Dr Lalchandani Lab, Jiya Eco Products, Sysco Industries, Schaeffler India, Escorts and many others. Here is what happened with the five major stocks that constituted a major part of my portfolio:

By the end of 2018, with the huge crash in the small-cap index, all these five stocks were deep in the red. MRSS and Focus Suites crashed 70–80 per cent; KP Energy and Lancer Container crashed 40–50 per cent; and Chemcrux was down 10 per cent. Many investors in the same situation might have sold off everything, and perhaps they might never have looked at the micro-cap space again. But I wanted to keep my emotions aside and make a rational decision. The biggest obstacle was the lack of data—there was no brokerage coverage, research reports or management guidance on those stocks.

So I visited all these companies' offices and factories in various cities, attended their AGMs and thoroughly searched the Internet to gather as much insight as possible on them. When a stock declines by as much as 40–50 per cent, that can either indicate an attractive entry opportunity for you or indicate that a greater fall is coming. Thus, knowing when to average (buy more) and when not to plays a very important role in your investment journey, which we will describe in detail in Chapter 5. After a thorough analysis of these five stocks, I took the following actions:

1. I made a complete exit from MRSS and Focus Suites at a loss of around 70 per cent, because my analysis revealed that these two stocks may not recover, but rather widen my losses further.
2. I held on to KP Energy and Lancer Container because both businesses hold a lot of potential and were only facing temporary headwinds during that time.
3. Throughout 2018, I increased my investment in Chemcrux, realizing that its business prospects had improved a lot while its valuation had turned much more attractive.

In hindsight, my decisions on these five stocks, except in the case of KP Energy, proved correct.

My income tax return filing revealed that in the financial year April 2018 to March 2019, my total loss amounted to more than Rs 1 crore! My unrealized losses from Lancer Container and KP Energy widened further in 2019. Only my position in Chemcrux Enterprises turned profitable, and I booked partial profits to fund some personal expenses and asset purchases. And even before the market had completely healed from the 2018 crash, COVID-19 triggered another major crash in 2020. Once again, my portfolio slid deep into the red. Things started looking better from the second half of 2020. After the pandemic, when the global container shortage issue grabbed the headlines, I increased my allocation in Lancer Container. The strategy paid off nicely. Although Lancer Container did not generate any returns for four long years from 2017 to 2020, the stock price jumped by more than ten times in 2021 alone. On the other hand, by 2022, Chemcrux Enterprises was showing more than 40 times the returns from my initial investment in 2017!

Overall, stocks like Chemcrux Enterprises, Lancer Container, Sirca Paints, Gujarat Themis, Bajaj Healthcare and some others once again helped my portfolio generate multibagger returns. Now, I will address a question very frequently asked of me: 'How did you accumulate the initial capital for all these investments?'

1.3 The Capital Accumulation Journey

If you are a new investor struggling to make it big, the question that should come to your mind is how to accumulate capital in the very first place. We all know that it takes money to earn money in the stock market. If an investment of Rs 1000 generates 10 times returns, that turns into only Rs 10,000, but if Rs 10 lakh were to

multiply 10 times, then your returns would be Rs 1 crore!
The big question is, how do you get that Rs 10 lakh? Here
are a few options:

1. Bank loans or any sort of borrowing
2. An inheritance or capital from family members
3. Trading in futures and options to quickly build capital

Before exploring all these options, I will briefly summarize
my own capital accumulation journey:

Stage 1 (2010–2014): Stocks like Ajanta Pharma, Atul Auto,
PI Industries, Mayur Uniquoters and some others helped
my capital of Rs 1 lakh grow to around Rs 7–8 lakh. Being a
college student, I had no major expenses. I didn't withdraw
any significant capital. Any money I got, I invested in the
stock market fully.

Stage 2 (2014-2017): Regular cash flows from my book
helped me increase my investment in stocks, while income
from the advisory services took care of all my personal and
business expenses. During this period, stocks like Can
Fin Homes, Caplin Point Lab, Avanti Feeds, Suprajit
Engineering, Kovai Medical, SNL Bearings and Sanwaria
Consumers helped my capital of Rs 10 lakh grow to more
than Rs 1 crore. With additional capital investment over
the years, the portfolio touched the Rs 3-crore mark.

Stage 3 (2017–2022): I suffered a loss of around Rs 1 crore
during the 2018–19 period as stocks like MRSS, Focus

Suites, Jhandewalas Foods and Sysco Industries and others tanked. However, the forty times returns from Chemcrux Enterprises, the nine times returns from Lancer Container and the more than 100 per cent returns from stocks like Sirca Paints, Gujarat Themis Biosyn, Bombay Metrics Supply Chain and many others helped that Rs 2–3 crore turn into multiple crores. The key reason for this growth lay in my substantial allocation to Chemcrux. As the stock price moved up, and with an increasingly better outlook for the future, I kept increasing my allocation to it, making it the largest holding in my portfolio. The strategy worked out very well. In fact, the gains from Chemcrux and Lancer helped clear all my bank loans and essentially funded my flat, office property and Mercedes car!

A careful study of the three stages reveals that if you can multiply your capital nine to ten times thrice over any period, that will create wonders for you. I did that over a twelve-year period, but it is possible in fewer years too. This is nothing but another form of compounding.

'Starting with Rs 1 lakh, if you can multiply your capital by ten times thrice then Rs 1 lakh turns into Rs 10 crore!'

Now, let's explore the options I listed for initial capital accumulation:

Bank loans or any other form of borrowing

Banks mostly offer loans at interest rates of anywhere between 7 per cent and 10 per cent. The rate of interest will reduce if you have an excellent credit score and offer some sort of collateral (like property or gold, against which you will take the loan). Without any collateral, the interest rate might be higher, but still, one can get a loan at an interest rate of 10–12 per cent. This appears an attractive proposition—getting a loan at 10 per cent and earning 20–30 per cent on it from the stock market. As we are talking about multibagger stocks, the proposition can appear even more attractive. Theoretically, one can borrow Rs 1 crore to invest in multibagger stocks and turn that into Rs 3 crore over a four-year period. Even after repaying the principal and the 10–12 per cent annual interest over the four-year period, one can still be left with a profit of more than Rs 1 crore. However, this proposition looks great only on paper. You need to repay the loan in EMIs, which essentially means you will require monthly cash flows. Whether from trading or investing, it is almost next to impossible to generate a steady monthly income from the stock market. Even the best trader in the world would face dull phases. In some months the earnings can be great while in other months one could lose a lot of money. If the market enters a dull phase or moves in a very narrow range for a long period of time, then liquidity will dry up and EMI payments will pose a big challenge. Missing your EMIs will make a big dent in your credit score. In the worst-case scenario, an unfavourable market can cause big trading losses, and the EMI burden on top of it would make life miserable. I have noticed many traders going bankrupt and going through a lot of misery because they had made external borrowings. Only very few experienced and highly disciplined traders can succeed in the market using borrowed funds. For an amateur, it is a sure-shot way to invite misery. Thus, if you are a new market participant wishing to make it big, never, ever start with borrowed funds. If you have already made it big and have more than ten to fifteen years of experience in stock market investing, then you can experiment with borrowed funds.

'For beginners, investing in the market with borrowed funds is a very dangerous practice; it can be a double-edged sword. Avoid it, unless you have enough expertise, funds and a few decades of experience.'

Inheritance or getting initial capital from family members

Many investors start their journey with inherited capital. I don't think that's an advantage. When you start with Rs 10–20 lakh or a bigger amount, then two things can happen:

1. You will play conservatively to protect the capital first.
   OR
2. You will first lose a large chunk of capital in some investment misadventure and then turn conservative to protect the remaining capital.

In both cases, you can't fully utilize the multifold return opportunities in the stock market. I have noticed that an investor who starts with an initial capital of Rs 10–20 lakh and loses 40–50 per cent of it, shifts his focus to either large-cap stocks or some conservative mutual funds. On the other hand, the person who starts with an investment of Rs 50,000 or Rs 1 lakh can freely explore multiple options. In my initial days, I lost a few thousand rupees, but the loss never affected me as the amounts were quite small. I had no dependents and no monthly obligations back then. Starting with small amounts always helps, because any kind of setback can be quickly reversed. Thus, starting with a large sum of inherited wealth can't be an advantage for investors.

Can Trading Help to Quickly Accumulate Capital?

Many new entrants to the stock market jump into futures and options trading to quickly accumulate capital. Futures and Options (F&O) trading courses remain in high demand. There are a lot of free YouTube videos and screenshots on social media showing how some have made huge profits from it and encourage many market participants to do trading. It is true that by doing a few trades, one can earn multifold returns within a matter of just a few months. However, you won't often find a person who turned Rs 1 lakh into Rs 10 crore and maintained that Rs 10 crore net worth for decades solely by trading. A person with Rs 1 crore capital and multiple decades of experience can make money from F&O trading, but it is very difficult for a beginner with Rs 1 lakh capital to multiply that into Rs 1 crore from F&O trading. There are practical setbacks. Whether from trading or investing, you will not be able to find anywhere in the world any market participant recording 100 per cent success. This is because even after multiple successful trades, a single loss-making trade can completely erode past profits.

Here is a chart illustrating this:

	Starting Capital Rs	Profit/Loss per cent	End Value in Rs
1st quarter	1 lakh	100 per cent profit	2 lakh
2nd quarter	2 lakh	25 per cent profit	2.5 lakh
3rd quarter	2.5 lakh	100 per cent profit	5 lakh
4th quarter	5 lakh	50 per cent loss	2.5 lakh
5th quarter	2.5 lakh	50 per cent loss	1.25 lakh

As it is clear from the chart, despite three successful rounds of profit-making—of 100 per cent, 25 per cent and 100 per cent—two rounds of 50 per cent loss have eroded all the profits made. One can argue that profit made from F&O can be invested in multibagger stocks for long-term wealth creation while the trading capital can remain constant. Well, it requires high expertise and discipline, and is easier said than done. I didn't find enough examples of those who excel in both F&O trading as well as long-term multibagger investing. Only one person, Rakesh Jhunjhunwala, made it big in a similar fashion; the other well-known names like

Vijay Kedia, Ramdeo Agarwal, Radhakishan Damani, etc., made their fortune from investing only.

Now, you will raise the point that profits can be eroded completely in investing as well. The major difference is that with a capital of Rs 1 lakh, one can invest in eight to ten or more stocks, but with the same capital, one can't take ten or twelve F&O trading positions simultaneously. If you invest Rs 1 lakh in ten different stocks, then even if a few of them did badly, your overall portfolio can still turn out a multibagger.

Here is an illustration of diversification in investing:

	Investment Rs	Returns	Position Closure Value Rs
1st stock	10,000	7 times	70,000
2nd stock	10,000	3.5 times	35,000
3rd stock	10,000	2.5 times	25,000
4th stock	10,000	2.5 times	25,000
5th stock	10,000	Zero	10,000
6th stock	10,000	Zero	10,000
7th stock	10,000	Zero	10,000
8th stock	10,000	50 per cent loss	5,000
9th stock	10,000	50 per cent loss	5,000
10th stock	10,000	50 per cent loss	5,000
Total	1,00,000		2,00,000

In the table above, although three stocks in the portfolio generated a loss of 50 per cent each and another three didn't generate any returns at all, the seven-fold returns from the first stock made up for all these poor performers. This means that even if the majority of the stocks in your portfolio stock disappoint but one or two generate ten times the returns, then too your portfolio can become a multibagger. In fact, this has happened with me many times. From 2014 to 2017, the gains from Can Fin Homes and Caplin made up for all the losses in the portfolio; and then, during 2020–22, Chemcrux and Lancer did wonders for the overall portfolio.

Now, you can ask, what if all the ten stocks in your portfolio suffered a setback? Well, this would be an indication that you did not have enough knowledge and expertise in the first place. If you can avoid some big mistakes and possess some knowledge about the market, then it generally never happens that all ten of your investment stocks can be wealth destroyers.

It is clear that, with limited capital, you can't properly diversify your trading position, but you can certainly diversify your investment position by putting your money in multiple stocks. Without diversification, your portfolio will carry a very high volatility risk. A single loss-making trade can erode gains from multiple profitable trades. This is the reason why beginners often fail to accumulate capital from trading. Successful traders must possess a relatively higher capital base or multiple and different sources of income. From my personal experience, I can say that it is relatively easier to accumulate capital from investing but very difficult to do so from trading. Once you possess a relatively larger capital base, then you can experiment in trading with the capital that you can afford to lose.

So far, I have only shared the names of the multibagger stocks that multiplied my portfolio several times. From the next chapter onwards, we will learn the secrets and triggers behind multibagger stocks. Let's explore!

Chapter 2

The Only Formula of Multibaggers

2.1 Introduction

Owning a stock is nothing but partial ownership of the business. When you invest in a stock, you become the owner of that business in equal proportion to the shares you have in that company. For example, if Reliance Industries has 5 billion shares in the market and you purchase one share of the company, then you own one five-billionths of Reliance Industries. So, even if you invest in just one share of Reliance, you have ownership of the company in proportion to that, which gets you voting rights. So, going by this straightforward ownership equation, one can conclude that:

> *'If the business grows by 10 per cent then the stock price should also grow by 10 per cent; or if the business drops by 20 per cent then the stock price should also drop by 20 per cent.'*

Correct?

However, in the stock market, this is always not the case! Business growth is not directly proportional to stock price growth! You can consider business growth by any parameter, like sales growth, profit growth, EPS (earnings per share) growth or anything else. Mostly, you will find that it does not match the stock price movements. Let's explore some real-life examples.

Example 1

ITC—Business Growth vs Stock Price Movement

Established in 1910, ITC is considered one of the finest Indian business conglomerates, with diverse business interests ranging from FMCG products, hotels and cigarettes to paper products. The company has maintained its debt-free status for the last twenty years, with the business generating free cash flows year after year. The last ten-year average return on equity (ROE) has been maintained at more than 25 per cent. However, despite being such a fine business with a strong balance sheet, the stock price return does not match the company's business growth!

Table 2.1: ITC, Earnings vs Stock Price Movement

	March 2017	March 2018	March 2019	2-year growth
Annual Net Profit	Rs 10,289 cr	Rs 11,271 cr	Rs 12,592 cr	22.38 per cent
Annual EPS	Rs 8.47	Rs 9.24	Rs 10.27	21.25 per cent
Stock Price (Average)	280	265	270	-3.57 per cent

(Stock price and EPS as per March 2019 data; if the stock undergoes split/bonus after this date, then the data will have to be adjusted accordingly)

So, over a two-year period, while the company's net profit jumped by 22 per cent, the stock price generated negative returns! You can consider sales growth during the same period, which too does not match with the stock price returns! And it is not just for this two-year period. Take any time period and you will find that the stock price movement is not in sync with the company's business growth!

Example 2

Dilip Buildcon—Earnings vs Stock Price Movement

Now, let's consider a 'not so strong' company that is unlike ITC. Dilip Buildcon is an infrastructure developer known for executing various road projects via Government of India tenders. Being a capital-intensive business, high debt was always a concern for the company. Its balance sheet quality and cash flow statements were always questionable. Let's have a look at the correlation between business growth and stock price returns in the case of this company.

As it is evident from the chart, although profit dropped by only 5 per cent over FY2018–19, the stock price crashed by 56 per cent. The investor can point out that the business is not doing as badly as the stock price indicates! You can compare sales growth or any other parameter over any period of time, and you will get similar results.

Table 2.2: Dilip Buildcon, Earnings vs Stock Price Movement

	March 2018	March 2019	Growth
Annual Net Profit	Rs 578 cr	Rs 547 cr	–5.36 per cent
Annual EPS	Rs 42.23	Rs 40.03	–5.21 per cent
Stock Price	980	430	–56.12 per cent

(Stock price and EPS as per March 2019 data; if the stock undergoes split/bonus after this date then the data will have to be adjusted accordingly)

Example 3

Reliance Industries—Earnings vs Stock Price Movement

Now let's consider the largest Indian company by market capitalization, Reliance Industries, which is the most tracked company among the research analyst community. Even for such a large and widely tracked business, stock price returns do not match with business growth!

As it is evident from Table 2.3, although net profit jumped by 32 per cent over the two-year period, the stock price jumped by 117 per cent! Clearly, the stock price movement is not in sync with the company's business growth.

Table 2.3: Reliance Industries, Earnings vs Stock Price Movement

	March 2017	March 2018	March 2019	Growth
Annual Net Profit	Rs 29,901 cr	Rs 36,075 cr	Rs 39,588 cr	32.40 per cent
Annual EPS	Rs 50.52	Rs 60.92	Rs 66.8	32.22 per cent
Stock Price	620	920	1350	117.74 per cent

(Stock price and EPS as per March 2019 data; if the stock undergoes split/bonus after this date, then the data will have to be adjusted accordingly)

Example 4

Chemcrux Enterprises—Business Growth vs Stock Price Movement

All the previous examples are from the large-cap and mid-cap space. Now, let's have a look at a micro-cap stock, Chemcrux Enterprises, from which I have earned more than forty times returns (as of 2022) and am still holding the stock at the time of writing this book.

Table 2.4: Chemcrux Enterprises, Earnings vs Stock Price Movement

	March 2019	March 2020	March 2021	March 2022	Growth
Sales	Rs 55 cr	Rs 57 cr	Rs 53 cr	Rs 95 cr	72 per cent
Annual Net Profit	Rs 9.3 cr	Rs 10.6 cr	Rs 8.9 cr	Rs 14.9 cr	60 per cent
Annual EPS	Rs 6.3	Rs 7.1	Rs 6.03	Rs 10.08	60 per cent
Stock Price	28	22	48	153	446 per cent

(Stock price and EPS as per March 2022; if the stock undergoes split/bonus after this date, then the data will have to be adjusted accordingly)

As it is clear from Table 2.4, from FY2019 to FY2022, total sales grew by 72 per cent, and both net profit and EPS jumped by 60 per cent. However, the stock price jumped by 446 per cent! There is a massive mismatch between the stock price movement and business growth!

So, whether a stock is a large-cap, mid-cap, small-cap or micro-cap, the result is the same. You can choose a random stock and compare its price movement with the business growth of the company, and you will get similar results. Not only that, you will sometimes even find that just after the company has posted a quarterly loss, the stock price has moved up; or that despite a business reporting record profits in a particular financial year, the stock price has dropped by a few percentage points!

2.2 Isn't the Stock Market All about Gambling?

If we summarize the previous section, it can be as follows:

- **ITC**—Despite business growth, its stock price showed marginal negative returns.
- **Dilip Buildcon**—The business did badly but the stock price crashed a lot more than the business de-growth warranted.
- **Reliance Industries**—Profitability improved by 32 per cent; however, the stock generated 117 per cent returns, again not in sync with the profit growth.
- **Chemcrux Enterprises**—Sales and profitability improved but the stock price of this micro-cap jumped a lot more, and was not in sync with the company's business growth.

Stock price movements are completely out of sync with the respective companies' business performance. In the case of some companies, the stock price rises a lot more than sales and profit growth do, and in the case of others, it is just the opposite. There might be one out of a thousand instances where the stock price moved exactly in sync with business growth (that too for a limited time period, not forever); but, as that happens one out of a thousand times we can safely assume that such an occurrence is an exception.

An important question will now come to your mind: As stock price returns are not directly proportional to the sales/profit growth, isn't stock market investing all about gambling? When an investor correlates business growth parameters with stock price movement, then he is likely to conclude that the entire stock market is a place for gambling and that those who have made it big in it have simply been lucky.

> *'A lot of individuals consider stock market investing as gambling because stock price movement is not directly proportional to business (sales or profit) growth.'*

Soon, I will reveal the missing link that most individuals who think this way are unaware of. But first let me clarify that if investing in equity were another form of gambling, then there cannot be so many billionaires across the world who made their fortunes from it. In gambling activities like card games or betting, you can win once, twice or thrice, but sooner or later, you will lose big. Check the list of billionaires and millionaires across the world on Wikipedia and follow their profession/source of wealth. None of them created fortunes from card games or betting, but many of them are equity investors. In India itself, there are many veteran investors like Rakesh Jhunjhunwala, Vijay Kedia, Ramdeo Agarwal, Ashish Kacholia and Dolly Khanna who have been consistently earning big from the stock market over the last few decades. If equity investing were another form of gambling, then one cannot make money consistently from it over the long run. So, while stock price movements are not in step with business growth, there must be a missing link that most individuals fail to interpret. Let's explore this missing link.

2.3 The Missing Link

The price-to-earnings (PE) ratio is a widely used valuation matrix in the stock market. Here is the formula for calculating it:

PE Ratio = Stock Price/Earnings per Share (EPS)

In other words, we can say that Stock Price = Earnings Per Share (EPS) × PE Ratio.

It simply means that the stock price is the function of both EPS and the PE ratio. EPS is calculated as a company's profits divided by the number of shares. Thus, mere earnings (profit) growth is not sufficient for stock price appreciation. Let's explore some examples to illustrate this.

Table 2.5: ITC, Earnings vs Stock Price Movement

	March 2017	March 2018	March 2019	2-year Growth
Annual Net Profit	Rs 10,289 cr	Rs 11,271 cr	Rs 12,592 cr	22.38 per cent
Annual EPS	Rs 8.47	Rs 9.24	Rs10.27	21.25 per cent
Stock Price	280	265	270	−3.57 per cent
PE Ratio	38.18	31	30	−21.42 per cent

(Stock price and EPS as per March 2019 data; if the stock undergoes split/bonus after this date, then the data will have to be adjusted accordingly)

As we can notice from the table, over the two-year period, although EPS jumped by 21 per cent, the PE ratio for the stock also contracted by a similar 21 per cent, resulting in marginally negative returns from the stock. Once you combine both earnings growth and the PE ratio, then you can get the rationale of stock price movement.

Table 2.6: Dilip Buildcon, Earnings vs Stock Price Movement

	March 2018	March 2019	Growth
Annual Net Profit	Rs 578 cr	Rs 547 cr	−5.36 per cent
Annual EPS	Rs 42.23	Rs 40.03	−5.21 per cent
Stock Price	980	430	−56.12 per cent
PE Ratio	37	13	−64.86 per cent

(Stock price and EPS as per March 2019 data; if the stock undergoes split/bonus after this date, then the data will have to be adjusted accordingly)

In the case of Dilip Buildcon, although earnings de-grew by 5 per cent, the PE ratio contracted by more than 60 per cent. The combined effect of both PE contraction and earnings de-growth resulted in a big crash in the stock price.

Table 2.7: Reliance Industries, Earnings vs Stock Price Movement

	March 2017	March 2018	March 2019	2-year Growth
Annual Net Profit	Rs 29,901 cr	Rs 36,075 cr	Rs 39,588 cr	32.40 per cent
Annual EPS	Rs 50.52	Rs 60.92	Rs 66.8	32.22 per cent
Stock Price	620	920	1350	117.74 per cent
PE Ratio	13	15.5	20.7	59.23 per cent

(Stock price and EPS as per March 2019 data; if the stock undergoes split/bonus after this date, then the data will have to be adjusted accordingly)

As revealed in Table 2.7, in the case of Reliance Industries, earnings registered a growth of 32 per cent while the PE ratio expanded by 59 per cent, which resulted in a jump of around 117 per cent in the stock price.

Table 2.8: Chemcrux Enterprises, Earnings vs Stock Price Movement

	March 2019	March 2020	March 2021	March 2022	Growth
Sales	Rs 55 cr	Rs 57 cr	Rs 53 cr	Rs 95 cr	72 per cent
Annual Net Profit	Rs 9.3 cr	Rs 10.6 cr	Rs 8.9 cr	Rs 14.9 cr	60 per cent
Annual EPS	Rs 6.3	Rs 7.1	Rs 6.03	Rs 10.08	60 per cent
Stock Price	28	22	48	153	446 per cent
PE Ratio	4.4	3.1	7.9	15.18	245 per cent

(Stock price and EPS as per March 2022; if the stock undergoes split/bonus after this date, then the data will have to be adjusted accordingly)

Table 2.8 reveals a similar picture. Although Chemcrux Enterprises registered an earnings growth of 60 per cent, during the same period, its PE ratio expanded from 4.4 to 15.18, which resulted in multibagger returns from the stock.

The above four examples cover stocks across market capitalization. But whether it is a large-cap, small-cap or micro-cap stocks, the story is the same in every instance. You can pick any random share and combine stock price movement with earnings and the PE ratio to understand this clearly.

Hopefully, by now the logic behind stock price movement is clear to you. The stock market is not all about gambling. Despite some short-term randomness, every long-term price movement follows a rationale. Many investors cannot figure out the driving forces behind stock price movement and consider equity investing as gambling. The very few investors who do figure out these driving forces earn big.

2.4 The Only Formula Underlying Multibagger Stocks

If you observe any stock that generated multifold returns, you will find a clear expansion in both earnings and PE ratio. From 2017 to 2022, Chemcrux Enterprises generated more than forty times the return in my portfolio. During the same period, the company witnessed earnings expansion of six to seven times and the PE ratio jumped by more than thirteen times. Without the expansion in the PE ratio, the stock price would never have turned into a forty-bagger. Between 2017 and 2022, Lancer Container reported an almost thirteen-time jump in earnings, while the PE ratio expanded by more than 200 per cent. No wonder the stock price generated more than thirty times the return in the same period. The same goes for all of my multibagger stocks, such as Can Fin Homes, Caplin Point Lab, Ajanta Pharma, Sirca Paints, Atul Auto and Gujarat Themis Biosyn.

You can choose any random stock that generated multifold returns in any year and you will notice the same picture; both earnings and PE ratio expansion is a must for multibagger stocks. Kindly note that earning expansion refers to growth in earning per share (EPS), not profit growth because, in the event of equity dilution, profit growth won't translate into similar EPS growth.

2.5 Life Cycle of a Multibagger Stock

I have studied many stocks that have generated multibagger returns over the past few decades and have noticed that their life cycle follows a similar pattern. While investing, it is important to recognize which phase the stock is currently trading in. Proper identification of a stock's life cycle helps in fathoming the returns expectation. Overall, we can divide the life cycle of a stock into three phases, as follows:

1. Initial phase
2. Advancement phase
3. Maturity or declining phase

Let's understand each phase in detail with some examples from the Indian stock market.

1. Initial Phase

In the initial phase, the stock should command a market capitalization of less than Rs 500 crore. This is a boring time to be invested in the stock because the stock price can remain range-bound over a long period of time, sometimes even years. It will test your patience. However, if one can successfully identify the stock in this phase then the rewards are maximum. The risk-reward ratio will remain very high, because if the investment clicks, you will end up with multifold returns but if it does not, then despite a wait of several years you might end up with wealth destruction. The characteristics of this phase are as follows:

- Low liquidity, low average trading volumes. In the initial phase of a multibagger, it is not feasible to buy a few crores' worth of shares in a single day. Large-quantity buying requires spreading the purchase over a few days.

- You won't find any institutional name (mutual funds, foreign institutional investors [FIIs], etc.) in the company's shareholder list because of low liquidity.

- You won't find any media coverage, research report, etc., on the company in the public domain as big names are yet to discover the stock.

- Valuation remains cheap at this stage. All the traditional valuation metrics, like PE ratio, PB ratio, etc., remain low compared with those of the company's peers.

- Despite improving fundamentals, you won't notice any significant price movement in this phase. The company might report back-to-back good quarterly performance; still the stock price may not respond accordingly, which will test your patience.

- It is the most difficult task to discover a potential multibagger in this phase. Moreover, after investment, it is even more difficult to hold the stock for an appropriate time frame.

Remember, social media coverage is one of the most important parameters in the initial phase of a potential multibagger stock. Nowadays, social media platforms such as Twitter, Facebook, YouTube and Telegram play a very important role in stock discovery. After shortlisting a stock, you should first do a Google search and then comb Twitter, Facebook, Telegram, YouTube, etc., to figure out the chatter about the stock. Despite the stock's low market capitalization and zero institutional shareholding, if you find that a lot of market participants are sharing buy/ sell comments, writing long notes and expressing their views on the stock, then the stock is no more in the initial phase. Either it has entered the advancement phase or will soon move into the declining phase. Obviously, at any point in time, there must be a certain number of market participants that are tracking and discussing the stock on various forums. All you need to do is to track the stock to see whether there is any 'excess optimism' or not. If there is a large number of players creating excessive buzz, advising you to purchase the stock on a regular basis, then it's time to be cautious.

The second most important point that you need to remember is that not all stocks move from the initial phase to the advancement phase. If that were the case, then anyone can earn multibagger returns just by investing in stocks of less than Rs 500 crore in market capitalization. There are thousands of stocks available in the market with a market capitalization of less than Rs 500 crore, and every year forty to eighty companies get listed on the SME exchange and may be considered as being in the 'initial phase' of their life cycle. Out of these thousands of stocks, maybe less than 1 per cent enter the next phase and generate multibagger returns for investors.

Examples:

1. Chemcrux Enterprises was in the initial phase of the multibagger life cycle during the April 2017-to-March 2021 period, and at the time of my writing this book, entered the advancement phase.
2. Page Industries was in the initial phase of the multibagger life cycle from 2007 to 2009, moved into the advancement phase, remained there from 2010 to 2017 and then passed into the mature phase.
3. Bharti Airtel was in the initial phase of the multibagger life cycle during the 2003–04 period, afterwards moved into the advancement phase, where it remained from 2004 until 2007 and from 2008 onwards has been in the mature phase.

2. *Advancement Phase*

From the initial phase, the stock enters the advancement phase once market capitalization and liquidity improve— or, in other words, until the stock price jumps significantly. This is still not too late to take a position on a multibagger stock after proper analysis. The characteristics of this phase are as follows:

• Liquidity improves, the average trading volume should be at least more than double that of the initial stage.

Gradually, with improved liquidity, it is possible to invest a few crores within a few days.

• We cannot put any strict market capitalization criteria for this phase. However, market capitalization too should have at least doubled from the previous phase, i.e., the stock price must have generated more than double returns from the first phase.

• Whenever the stock price generates more than double returns with increased trading volume, it grabs the attention of institutional investors (mutual funds, FIIs). Big investors start taking positions in the stock, which triggers another round of multifold returns at this stage.

• With the entry of institutional investors, media coverage and research reports start pouring in. More and more retail investors are now getting attracted to the story.

• The scope for PE expansion still remains bright. Over this period, the valuation gets re-rated, helping the stock to generate multifold returns.

• Due to a significant increase in the stock price, the company no longer remains an unknown name among market participants. Self-proclaimed analysts start making YouTube videos and posting on Twitter about the bright prospects of the company.

The most important point that you need to remember is that not every stock that enters the advancement phase moves into the mature phase. Many stocks directly enter the declining phase that destroys wealth. Thus, the advancement phase offers a quick money-making opportunity only if the investor can time his or her entry and exit properly. Maximum PE expansion is noticed in this phase. In some cases, the valuation enters an unsustainable range, which triggers stock price correction. Investment in the stock during this period still remains tricky, because you can either quickly make multifold gains or make a big loss.

Examples:

1. Chemcrux Enterprises was in the initial phase of the multibagger life cycle from April 2017 to March 2021. From April 2021, over the next fifteen months, the stock price increased by more than five times. Liquidity improved a lot and more market participants started discussing the stock. Thus, despite the low market capitalization, we can safely say that after April 2021 the stock entered the advancement phase. Entry of institutional investors (mutual funds, portfolio management services [PMS], FIIs, etc.) is still pending at the time of writing this book. Only time can tell how long this advancement phase in Chemcrux will last.

2. Page Industries generated around thirty times the return on investment during the advancement phase of its multibagger life cycle, from 2010 to 2017.

3. Bharti Airtel generated around sixty times the return on investment during the advancement phase of the multibagger life cycle, from 2004 to 2007.

As is evident from the examples, the advancement phase offers opportunities for maximum returns. In a few instances, more than 100 times returns have been observed during this phase as a result of exponential PE expansion backed by earnings growth.

3. *Mature Phase, or Declining Phase*

Few shares move from the advancement to the mature phase. Some move into the declining phase. Whichever way the stock moves, by this time the stock becomes the talk of the town. After the huge returns it has generated, the stock is now well-known to all market participants. At this stage, you will find media headlines like, 'An investment of Rs 1000 in stock X is now worth 1 crore'. Such headlines attract new investors, and they jump into the scene. Remember, investment during this phase often fails to generate multifold returns. There can be two possibilities:

1. 10–20 per cent compounded annual growth in stock price continues (mature phase)
2. Wealth destruction (declining phase)

The characteristics of a stock in the mature phase are as follows:

- High liquidity and trading volumes. The stock enters into a frontline index like the NIFTY 50 or NIFTY 500.
- High recognition in the market and lots of media attention, research reports and public interest.
- Significant institutional holding (by FIIs or mutual funds) in the shareholding pattern.
- The business continues its earnings growth. At this stage, the business can withstand a few external shocks.
- The stock is already traded at a higher valuation. Thus, despite earnings growth, PE expansion is no longer visible.

Examples:

1. After generating thirty times the return on investment from 2010 to 2017, Page Industries entered into the mature phase from 2018 onwards. You will notice that from FY2018 till date, the company's earnings growth has continued. However, in the absence of PE expansion, the stock failed to generate another round of five to ten times the returns.

2. Bharti Airtel entered the mature phase in 2008. In the absence of consistent earnings growth, the stock mostly remained range bound for thirteen long years, from 2008 to 2020. Back in 2007, stories about how an investment of Rs 1 lakh in the stock turned into Rs 60 lakh filled the media. Investors who took inspiration from those stories and bought the stock didn't earn anything for the next thirteen years!

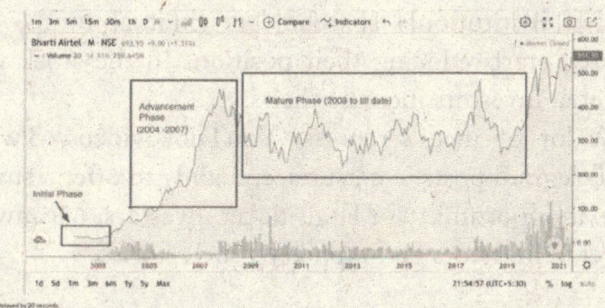

Fig. 2.1: Multibagger Life Cycle of Bharti Airtel

Declining Phase

This is the most dangerous stage of the multibagger life cycle. Most investors who invest at this stage lose money. The characteristics of this phase are as follows:

- As in the mature phase, the stock commands high liquidity and trading volumes. A lot of media attention, research reports, etc., surface around it.
- Unlike in the mature phase, the business fails to deliver earnings growth, and as a result, the PE ratio starts contracting.
- A combination of declining earnings growth and PE contraction results in an exponential fall in the stock price.
- During its fall, occasional pullback rallies bring hope; however, such pullback rallies later prove to be traps.
- One of the most distinctive features of this phase is that institutional shareholders (mutual funds, FIIs, etc.) start reducing their positions in the stock while retail investors increase theirs.
- A lot of media reports, YouTube videos, Twitter, Telegram posts, etc., surface, mainly to offer a smooth exit opportunity for large-ticket investors. Meanwhile, retail investors get trapped by such stories.

During the advancement phase, many stocks experience 8–10 times or even higher PE ratio expansion very quickly. Generally, it is noticed that after such a huge valuation expansion, the stock quickly enters the declining phase, causing 80–95 per cent value erosion. Moreover, after this

90 per cent erosion, it becomes almost impossible for the stock to regain its previous heights.

Examples:

During 2018, I was trapped in stocks like MRSS and Focus Suites in their declining phase. I invested in both stocks during the late advancement phase and suffered a massive loss of around 70 per cent while the stocks rapidly entered the declining phase. Over the years, I have come across hundreds of portfolios and have noticed how investors lost massive sums from investing in stocks like Suzlon, Educomp, Unitech, JP Associates, Yes Bank, etc., buying them in the declining phase.

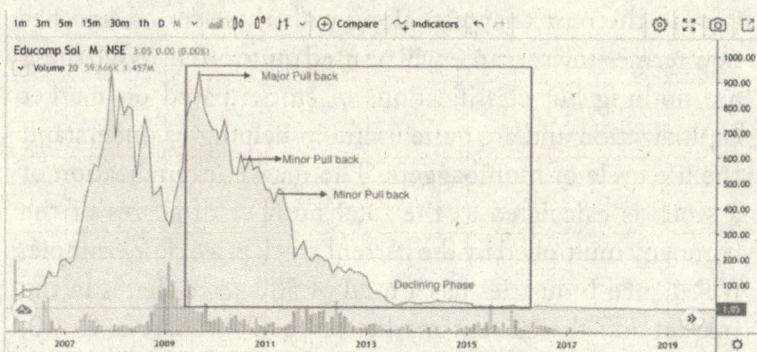

Fig. 2.2: Declining phase of Educomp

As we can see from Fig. 2.2, Educomp generated around 18 times the return on investment during the 2006–07 period, supported by PE expansion. After that, with PE contraction and a decline in earnings, the stock

quickly entered the declining phase. There were occasional
pullback rallies across the 2009–11 period. But ultimately,
the stock continued its downward journey and crashed
into the single-digit range, destroying almost 95 per cent
of investor wealth. A quick look at the historical price
chart of once well-known stocks like Suzlon, JP Associates,
Unitech, etc., will reveal a similar story.

> 'Irrespective of the media coverage, positive news, etc., never
> invest in a stock that recently witnessed more than double PE ratio
> expansion. Such stocks can quickly prove to be wealth destroyers.'

You might have already observed that terms like large-cap,
mid-cap and small-cap are frequently used in this book. In
fact, in the next chapters, along with these terms, another
new term—micro-cap—will be used quite often. Well, these
are nothing but classifications of stocks based on market
capitalization and are quite useful in helping us understand
the life cycle of multibaggers. The market capitalization of
a stock is calculated as the total number of shares of the
company multiplied by the current stock price. For example,
if Reliance Industries has a total of 500 crore shares in the
market and the current market price of its share is Rs 10,
then its current market capitalization would be Rs 5,000
crore. If the stock price jumps from Rs 10 to Rs 30, then
the market capitalization would jump to Rs 15,000 crore.
The total number of shares mostly remains fixed (except
during a few instances of equity dilution). Thus, market
capitalization keeps multiplying while a stock moves ahead

in its multibagger life cycle. Based on market capitalization, we can divide stocks into the following categories:

1. **Micro-cap stocks**: Stocks that have a market capitalization of less than Rs 500 crore. At this stage, the stock remains in the initial phase of the multibagger life cycle. Companies that are coming out with initial public offerings (IPO) on the BSE SME and NSE SME stock exchanges start their journey as micro-cap stocks.

2. **Small-cap stocks**: They have a market capitalization of between Rs 500 crore and Rs 5000 crore. Many small-cap stocks remain in the initial phase of the multibagger life cycle. If a micro-cap stock quickly enters into the small-cap zone, then we can say it is in the advancement phase, and it will most likely graduate to the mid-cap stage also. The micro-cap and small-cap phases are the ideal stages for multibagger discovery for maximum wealth creation.

3. **Mid-cap stocks**: They have a market capitalization of between Rs 5000 crore and Rs 20,000 crore. When a small-cap stock enters the mid-cap zone, we can safely say that the stock is now in the advancement phase of the multibagger life cycle. The stock price appreciates the most during this phase. On the contrary, while a stock enters the declining phase, it turns from large-cap to mid-cap and then small-cap, destroying investor wealth.

4. **Large-cap stocks:** These stocks are over Rs 20,000 crore in market capitalization. These are generally the top 100 largest companies listed on the stock market.

A few large-cap stocks have had a market capitalization of more than Rs 20,000 crore from the day of their listing. Some of them are LIC, Paytm (One97 Communication), Coal India, etc. But a large number of stocks have gone through the stages of the complete multibagger life cycle before entering this mature phase and are now termed large-cap. Examples of such stocks are Infosys, Wipro, HDFC Bank, Asian Paints and Page Industries. All these stocks generated huge wealth along their journey from small-cap to large-eap.

Kindly note that there is no strict classification that determines whether a stock is large-cap, mid-cap, small-cap and micro-cap. It can keep changing from time to time. Further, what is a large-cap in the Indian context can be a mid-cap on the NASDAQ (a US stock market). All these terms are relative in nature and can keep changing.

'Micro-cap' is a relatively new term. There are indices based on large-cap, mid-cap and small-cap stocks, but there has been nothing such as a micro-cap index so far. So, remember that these terms are used for reference purposes only.

'For multibagger returns, identification of quality micro-cap and small-cap stocks during their initial phase, with both earnings and PE expansion potential, should remain the target.'

Chapter 3

Multibagger Stock Selection

3.1 Introduction

So far, we have obtained a clear idea about the life cycle of a multibagger stock. It is of utmost importance to invest in it in the initial phase to reap maximum benefits from it. The stock remains relatively unknown at this stage, making it difficult for research and analysis. Most market participants are completely unaware of the stock. Remember, there are always thousands of little-known micro-cap stocks available in the market. It is not like you can invest in any one of them at random and can earn multifold returns. In fact, out of thousands of such lesser-known micro-cap stocks, less than 1 per cent generate multibagger returns and the remaining turn out to be wealth destroyers. Once a micro-cap or small-cap stock consistently experiences earnings and PE expansion, then it generates huge wealth for investors. Thus, before investing in any stock, you should have a clear idea about triggers that can expand earnings and PE multiples, both. Earnings expansion alone is not sufficient for multibagger returns. Similarly, without earnings growth, PE expansion won't last for very long. Thus, potential multibagger stock selection requires a clear understanding of the triggers that can fuel both earnings and PE expansion. In the next section, I will first describe those triggers and then share case studies of both wealth destruction and multibagger returns from my portfolio stocks.

3.2. Triggers for Multibagger Stocks

Trigger #1: Margin Expansion

Margin expansion is the first and foremost trigger for both earnings and PE ratio growth. Generally, you will find two different kinds of margins on financial websites:

1. **EBITDA Margin**: It measures how much in earnings (profit) a company has generated before interest, taxes, depreciation and amortization as a percentage of its revenue. EBITDA Margin = EBITDA / Revenue. This margin is also referred to as the 'operating profit margin'.
2. **Net Profit Margin**: This measures how much profit is generated as a percentage of revenue. So Net Profit Margin = Net Profit/ Revenue (Total Sales)

Under ideal circumstances, both margins should run in sync—i.e., if the EBITDA margin keeps improving then the net profit margin should also improve, and vice-versa. EBITDA stands for earnings before interest, tax, depreciation and amortization, so if any one of these parameters shows some anomaly, then it will reflect on both margins.

Remember, the net profit margin in absolute terms says nothing about the prospects of a stock. A business with a net profit margin of 15 per cent may or may not be a better bet than a business with a 10 per cent net profit margin. It is the trend that decides stock price movement, here the keyword is **"trend"**. If the margin expands from 10 per cent to 15 per cent over a period of a few years, then the PE ratio must expand and the stock price should follow. This association applies in the case of margin contraction too. Every wealth destroyer has experienced margin contraction over the long term.

While hunting for multibagger stocks, the criteria for selecting them should follow this order of preference:

1. Visibility of both EBITDA and net profit margin expansion for the business.
2. The business's ability to protect its margins across different economic cycles. In other words, its profit margin should not experience wild volatility.
3. Visibility of margin contraction is a negative criterion, and such businesses should be avoided.

You will find that historically, over a period of five to ten years, out of thousands of stocks, very few businesses demonstrate a range-bound margin trend, while most others demonstrate high volatility in the margin. Now we will discuss the three drivers behind margin expansion and contraction:

1. Pricing power of the business.
2. Backward integration
3. Industry tailwinds

Pricing Power

While we say a business has some pricing power, it means that the company can pass on any kind of raw material price hike to the end customer or has strong negotiation powers when it comes to its suppliers or customers. In either case, the company can protect its net profit margin. Broadly, depending on the end customer, all businesses can be categorized under one of the following two models:

1. **B2B model**: B2B refers to 'business to business'. A B2B company provides services or products to other businesses. For example, a bottle manufacturer sells bottles to other businesses like liquor companies or pharma companies.
2. **B2C model**: B2C refers 'business to customer'. A B2C company directly sells services or products to the end customer. For example, liquor manufacturers or drug manufacturers can directly sell their end products to the customer.

Remember, a business can have a presence in both B2B and B2C segments—such as tyre manufacturers (MRF, Apollo Tyres), who cater directly to customers in the replacement market and supply to auto companies like Maruti, Hyundai and Tata Motors as well. Also, within an industry segment like FMCG or pharma, some players may have a presence in B2B and some in B2C. So, an in-depth understanding of the business value chain is required to discover whether a business is in the B2B or B2C segment.

B2C companies always remain in an advantageous position when it comes to their ability to protect their margins because it is always easier to negotiate with retail customers than with other large businesses. When you purchase medicines manufactured by Abbott or GSK, can you negotiate with them? In fact, the scope for negotiation at pharmacy stores is almost non-existent. However, companies like Abbott India can easily negotiate with their suppliers. So the businesses (packaging companies, active pharmaceutical ingredient (API) players, etc.) supplying to Abbott are of the B2B model and have no pricing power. But Abbott itself is in the B2C segment and has a lot of pricing power. Naturally, if you examine the historical margins of Abbott India, you will find a very strong and consistent margin trend.

Net Profit Margin Annual % of Abbott India Ltd.

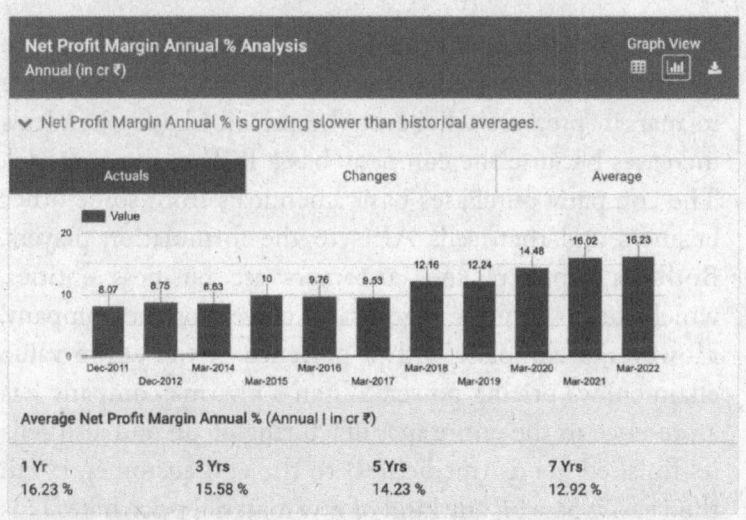

Fig. 3.1: Abbott India, Historical Net Profit
Margin Trend

Not surprisingly, Abbott India has created a lot of wealth for investors over the last five to ten years. Over the last ten years, the stock price has gained by more than thirteen times, while in the last five years, the stock price has risen by more than five times.

Backward Integration

A business that has executed backward integration has a presence in the entire value chain of the industry it operates in. Here is the value chain of a medicines manufacturer:

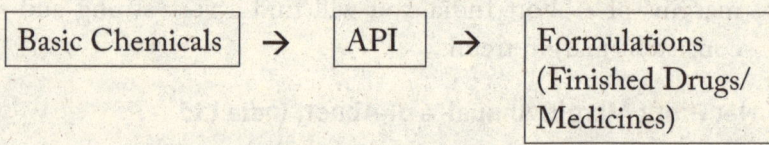

A pharma company that has a presence only in the active pharmaceutical ingredient (API) segment is vulnerable to margin pressure whenever the price of basic chemicals increases because the company has a B2B business model. The company purchases basic chemicals from some other business and then sells APIs to the formulation players. Both its suppliers and customers are business entities, which means limited negotiation power for the company. However, a company with a presence in the entire value chain enjoys pricing power. When a pharma company has a presence in the entire manufacturing chain and also sells its finished goods (medicines) to the end customer, it can then easily pass on any kind of raw material price hike. This pharma company's customers can't negotiate much when they purchase its medicines, and this means such players enjoy pricing power.

Overall, it is easier for a fully backward integrated company with a B2C business model to pass on any kind of raw material price hike. During adverse external situations, such companies can protect their margins, and in favourable situations they can expand their profit margins, paving the way for multibagger returns for their investors.

> '*A fully backward integrated business with a B2C model is the best candidate as a potential multibagger stock.*'

Industry Tailwinds

Suppose you are an exporter of basmati rice to countries in the Middle East like Saudi Arabia, the UAE, Iran, Oman or Kuwait and currently have huge stocks of rice in your inventory. All of a sudden, due to some reasons, the demand in these countries for basmati rice increases manifold. Now you can easily sell your existing stocks (rice) at a much higher price than might otherwise have been possible. Everything else remains the same, but the selling price has zoomed, helping you to earn higher margins. This phenomenon can be called an 'industry tailwind'. Normally, such situations are out of your control and can't be predicted. For example, one of my multibagger stocks, Lancer Container, enjoyed a massive industry tailwind in the period from late 2020 to 2021. Following the COVID-19 pandemic, there was a global container shortage, which sent freight rates skyrocketing. Lancer capitalized on the opportunity and its net profit margin zoomed from 3.13 per cent in the quarter ending September 2020 to 5.24 per cent in the quarter ending December 2021. This huge jump in its profit margin helped the stock price generate more than ten times returns in 2021 alone. Remember, even a 1 percentage point jump in margin is huge from the perspective of multibagger returns. The only point you need to remember is that sooner or later the industry tailwind will reverse, so you need to time your exit from such stocks properly.

> 'Industry tailwinds can't be predicted beforehand; it should not be the sole investment rationale. In the presence of all other multibagger triggers, industry tailwinds accelerate the multibagger returns.'

Overall, net profit margin is the most crucial deciding factor for multibagger returns. Let us now understand in detail the other triggers that have a bearing on earning expansion or contraction.

Trigger #2: Debt

If margin expansion is the first and foremost parameter for multibagger returns, then the second most important deciding factor is the debt burden or the quantum of borrowing in the company's books of accounts. In fact, the profit margin can expand or contract depending on the debt burden of the company.

Suppose the net profit of two businesses, A and B, is Rs 100 each. Both companies are desirous of growing their profit by 100 per cent within the next two years. Business

A is in software development and can grow with minimal investments. Just by hiring a little more talent, it can achieve the target. The cash generated from its day-to-day business is enough to support these minimal investments, and thus the company won't require any external borrowings. Business B is in infrastructure development. It bags orders by participating in government tenders. It needs external borrowings to grow its business. On the one hand, business A requires no bank loans for growth, and on the other, business B requires loans for growth. As an investor, if you have the choice to invest in any one of these two businesses, which one would you choose?

Even if both businesses can double their earnings at a similar pace, business A would be the first choice for investment because it does not need external borrowings to fund its growth. External borrowings mean that irrespective of the business cash flows, every month you need to repay something. We all know that at certain times every business can go through a rough phase. Suppose you are a hotel owner whose business was doing very well but all of a sudden the COVID-19 pandemic put the brakes on your business. When things will return to normal is out of your control. If you had opted for a huge bank loan to build the hotel, then the monthly loan repayment burden can easily leave you bankrupt. However, if you had zero loans and no monthly EMI burden, then no matter how long the pandemic lasts, you can easily survive and come back strong. Thus, while searching for multibaggers, a very important consideration would be the debt burden of the business. For this purpose, we will look at a target company's debt-to-equity ratio. This ratio is calculated by dividing the company's total liabilities by its total shareholder funds. The ratio is readily available on many financial websites so you don't have to burden yourself with manually calculating it every time you analyse a stock for its multibagger potential. We can divide companies into three categories on the basis of the following debt-to-equity ratios.

1. Debt-to-equity ratio of 0 to 0.3
2. Debt-to-equity ratio of 0.3 to 1
3. Debt-to-equity ratio of more than 1

Let's have a quick look at these three categories:

Companies with a debt-to-equity ratio of less than 0.3

Zero-debt companies are the safest investment options; they can't go bankrupt and are absolutely at zero risk of default. Irrespective of how unfavourable the external business environment is, such a business can survive for the longest possible period. You might wonder how a zero-debt company can grow. After all, earnings expansion is a must for multibagger returns, and for earnings expansions, a business requires capital investment. Well, there are many listed companies (mainly MNCs) that are growing consistently, maintaining their zero-debt status for years. They are doing so simply by reinvesting the cash generated from the business, instead of opting for external borrowing. It is also true that you won't easily find such companies. So, the second best option is to look for companies with minimal debt. We can safely consider companies as having minimal debt when their debt-to-equity ratio is less than 0.3. Overall, if a company satisfies all other criteria of earnings and PE expansion and has a debt-to-equity ratio of less than 0.3, then it can be a great potential multibagger stock.

Companies with a debt-to-equity ratio of 0.3 to 1

The range between 0.3 to 1 is still a fair zone to search for potential multibagger stocks. In such cases, we need to make sure that the overall debt level is not increasing year after year. If the interest coverage ratio remains above the comfort zone and the overall debt level decreases over a period of a few years, then that would be a good sign. Obviously, we need to consider all other remaining parameters for earnings and PE expansion and then only zero in on a stock as a potential multibagger.

Companies with a debt-to-equity ratio of more than 1

Companies in this category often possess stretched balance sheets and poor cash flows from operations. These companies are the most vulnerable during any economic downturn. Historically, if you carefully notice all the stocks that have crashed by more than 90 per cent, you will find that most of them had debt-to-equity ratios of more than 1. There are very few instances of such companies drastically reducing their debt burden and rewarding investors. I did a quick search and noticed that there are around 3000 companies with debt-to-equity ratios of less than 1. So, while searching for multibaggers, if we contain ourselves within this universe alone we have enough options to choose from.

Kindly note that for banking and financial stocks, the debt-to-equity ratio has no significance because money is the raw material for them. Banks accept customer deposits and use that money to extend loans and make profits. So, for banks, customer deposits are a liability, and the more of the liability (deposit) they have, the better their capacity to extend larger loans to earn higher profits. This is the reason why you will find high debt-to-equity ratios in banks and financial companies. It is safe to ignore this ratio for banks and financial companies.

Trigger #3: Capacity Expansion

Capacity expansion is a no-brainer option for revenue (total sales) growth. Suppose a company is generating a revenue of Rs 100 crore from a single-location factory. Now, if it expands capacity by setting up another, similar factory, then its revenue will easily double to Rs 200 crore. Correct? However, revenue growth is not a deciding factor for multifold returns from stocks. We have already seen in Chapter 2 that a stock can fail to deliver despite revenue growth in the absence of EPS and PE expansion. In a lot of other examples in this book, you will see stocks turning into wealth destroyers when their margins contract, despite their revenue growing. Thus, it is important to analyse whether any capacity expansion by a company will help in margin growth or not.

> '*Capacity expansion will always trigger revenue expansion but not always margin expansion. Thus, capacity expansion alone is not sufficient for multibagger returns from stocks.*'

Broadly, there are four ways by which a company expands capacity:

1. **Greenfield expansion**: Here a company develops capacity from scratch. So, land acquisition, building construction, machinery installation . . . everything becomes part of the expansion project. Naturally, such projects require huge investments and external borrowings. Large borrowings mean monthly repayments of the loans, which can restrict margin expansion.

2. **Brownfield expansion**: In this type of expansion, the project site is partly developed and the infrastructure is not required to be built from scratch. For example, the land is already acquired, the minimum required infrastructure is ready and now the company only requires to add some amenities to complete the project. Thus, compared with greenfield expansion, brownfield expansion requires less investment and fewer borrowings by the company. Obviously, because of the lower debt requirement, such expansions are preferred over the former.

3. **Modernization of machinery**: Capacity expansion is possible without any new building or factory construction. Within the same factory premises, the company replaces its old machinery with more modern ones so that output can increase. In such cases, no huge investment is required. Minimal debt or internal accruals are enough to fund such expenditure. The probability of margin contraction is minimal in such expansion, making it one of the preferred types of capacity expansion to look out for when spotting potential multibagger stocks.

4. **Change of product mix**: This is perhaps the best
    trigger for multibagger stocks. Nothing can be better
    if a company can increase capacity without any
    investment at all! Sounds unrealistic? Well, Chemcrux
    Enterprises, which is already a forty-bagger stock for
    me, chose this option to increase output. Time and
    again, the company would say they were a 'process-
    based' company so they could easily shift to products
    that are in high demand and can increase output that
    aids in margin expansion. From FY2017 to FY2019,
    the company's revenue soared from Rs 27 crore to Rs
    55 crore, its operating profit margin doubled from 13
    per cent to 26 per cent and its EPS rose by six times
    without the company having made any major capital
    investment. Afterwards, in FY2020 and FY2021, both
    margin and sales were affected by factory closure and
    COVID-related disruptions, but that is a different
    story. Here, the point to note is that if a company can
    expand capacity without any major investment, then
    that would be the best case for multibagger returns.

Overall, don't get enthusiastic about looking solely at the
capacity expansion plans of a company, as expansion can
go both ways. Only when the expanded capacity helps
the company to produce higher-margin products with
minimum leverage is it great news for investors.

Thus, whenever a company announces some mega
capacity expansion plan, instead of investing in the stock
outright, seek answers to the following questions:

1. What type of expansion is the company looking to
    make?

2.   How much investment is required to execute the project? Often, the term 'capex' (capital expenditure) is used to denote this amount.

3.   How will the company fund that capex? Will it do so from internal accruals or external borrowings?

4.   If from external borrowings, then how is it going to affect the company's debt-to-equity ratio? How much additional interest expense burden will it result in?

5.   Within how many years would it take for the added capacity to contribute to revenue?

Whenever some huge investment is required for capacity expansion, I prefer to opt out of the stock. There can be attention-grabbing news headlines, such as 'The company is planning for the largest-ever investment to set up the biggest factory in the world'. Such headlines can easily push up the stock price over the next few days. But remember—if the company falls into a debt trap while this huge expansion is on, then its stock price will nosedive. The bigger the investment in the project, the bigger will be the risk. To be on the safe side, I always prefer to invest in companies that embark on capacity expansion with minimal capex.

Trigger #4: Capitalization of opportunity size

A huge opportunity or a huge market size that will allow for expansion is a must for multibagger returns from stocks. Take the example of Coal India, the largest coal producer in the country. As the company already accounts for almost 80 per cent of the total coal production in the country, there is little chance that the company can double or triple its earnings in a few years. In fact, in the last ten years, the compound annual profit growth rate stands at only 2 per cent. Moving in step with this, the stock price has also disappointed over the last ten years. So, don't be under the impression that just because a company is government owned and the biggest in its segment, the stock price must generate good returns for investors. Very few who invested in Coal India after its 50–70 per cent price crash and timed their exit made good money, and they are exceptions. The majority lost money by investing in Coal India.

Among the parameters that influence stock performance, earnings growth is always preferred above anything else. Thus, an early-stage business with a huge opportunity size is always a preferred choice over a mature business like Coal India. However, you need to remember that huge market size cannot be the sole deciding factor for investment in a company. In the period 2007–11, the airline sector had a huge opportunity size. The market was ever-growing. More and more middle-class people were opting to fly rather than travel by train. However, Jet Airways and Kingfisher from among the largest airlines went bankrupt, while SpiceJet struggled a lot to survive. The stocks of these three airlines caused massive wealth destruction for investors. Companies like Suzlon had a huge addressable market in the renewable energy segment but Suzlon turned out to be one of the biggest wealth destroyers in the Indian market.

'Huge opportunity size is a must for multibagger returns. However, opportunity size alone should not be the deciding factor for investment.'

For multibagger returns, the business needs to capitalize on its opportunity size properly. Let's take an example to illustrate this. Rohit owns a packaged food start-up and mostly sells via e-commerce platforms such as Amazon, Flipkart and Jiomart. One of his packaged food items, a healthy snack, sells a lot and has received hundreds of good reviews within a month of its launch. With the encouraging response, Rohit decides to increase production for further market penetration. Incremental production from the same factory premises does not require huge investments; just increasing the number of shifts or hiring additional manpower would serve the purpose. Thus, internal accruals from the business itself can fund the expansion, and no external borrowings would be required. When this is the case, net profit growth for the business can remain in sync with the revenue growth.

Let's take another example. Mohit recently ventured into the hotels business and set up the first hotel in his locality. In the first year of its operations itself, the business did extremely well. Online reviews and word-of-mouth publicity did wonders for it, and the hotel is mostly fully booked. With this encouraging response, Mohit decided to establish another hotel in a nearby location. Another hotel means the business can quickly double its revenue. However, the jump in revenue is not likely to convert into a similar profit expansion. Setting up a hotel is a capital-intensive process that requires bank loans or external funding. The interest expenses would eat up the incremental revenue.

The opportunity size in both cases is large enough to bring business growth, and both companies can increase their revenue at a similar pace, but when it comes to earnings expansion, they will differ. Purely from an earnings expansion point of view, which one of the two businesses would you prefer? Obviously, it would be the first one, the packaged food business that capitalized on opportunity well.

Can Fin Homes is one such example from my multibagger stock list. The company mainly offers low-ticket-size home loans to individuals from the low- and middle-income segments, preferably the salaried class. Before 2013, the company had a limited presence in south India. However, from 2013 to 2017, the company went in for aggressive branch expansion. The opportunity size in the home loan segment was huge at that time, and even today remains so. Can Fin Homes had a strong loan book with low NPAs as it mainly catered to salaried individuals. When such a business expands its branch network aggressively with minimal investments, it always speaks well for the stock price. Despite its expansion, the company maintained its focus on individual borrowers who took low-ticket-size loans and thus maintained its low NPAs. If it had ventured into the corporate segment, then that would have cast a big shadow on its stock price performance.

Overall, one needs to remember that while huge opportunity size is a must for multibagger returns, at the end of the day, how a company capitalizes on that opportunity decides its multibagger journey.

Trigger #5: Geographical expansion of markets

If a company finds higher-margin markets in new geographies for its products, then that is a desirable trigger, indicating a potential multibagger stock. This unleashes earnings expansion without the concomitant debt that accompanies expansion otherwise. Caplin Point Lab was a prime example of a company that successfully expanded its market geographically. From FY2013 to FY2017, the company aggressively extended its sales operations in the semi-regulated markets of Latin America and several African countries. Due to the low level of competition in these markets and the better pricing power the company could enjoy there, it successfully expanded its profit margin from 7.6 per cent in FY2012 to 20.58 per cent in FY2017. In fact, the company's net profit margin expanded every year in those six years, which itself is a rare occurrence. India has a huge talent pool and the cost of manufacturing here is comparatively low in the global context. Thus, when a company manufactures in India and successfully penetrates the global market, it automatically opens up possibilities for margin expansion.

Net Profit Margin Annual % of Caplin Point Laboratories Ltd.

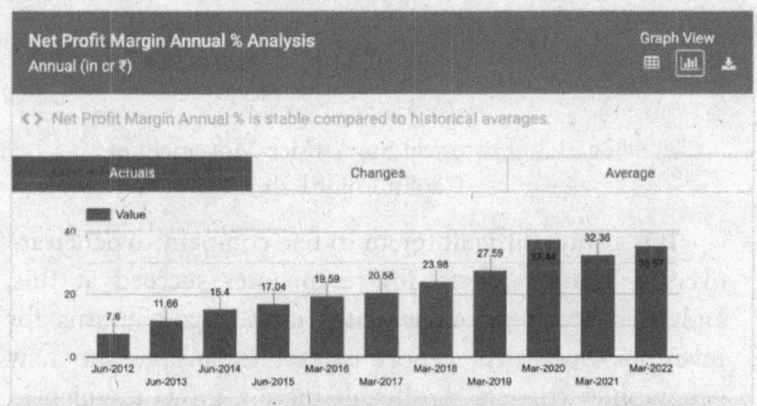

Fig. 3.2: Caplin Point Lab—Net Profit Margin, 2012–22

If you follow the stock price movement of Caplin Point Lab in Fig. 3.3, you will find that over the long run the stock price replicated the margin trend. From 2012 to 2017, the net profit margin more than doubled, expanding every year and resulting in net profit rising more than ten times. This helped the PE ratio to expand from the 10–11 level to the 50–55 level. As a result, in the same period, the stock price rose by more than 100 times! My investment from 2014 to 2016 yielded around 13 times the return. I made a complete exit in 2016 as I realized that the PE ratio may not expand further from the 45–50 level. Driven by the strong bull run in 2017, Caplin continued its upward journey that year, but from 2018 to 2020, the stock price declined.

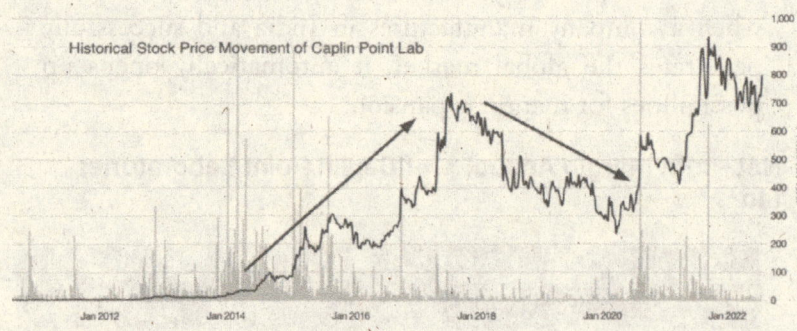

Fig. 3.3: Historical Stock Price Movement of
Caplin Point Lab

It is always difficult for an Indian company to penetrate overseas markets. Very few companies succeed at this, and their stock price generates multibagger returns for investors. Successful export market expansion into new geographies triggers significant margin growth, which in turn helps drive earnings and PE expansion, paving the way for multibagger returns. During 2021–22, I had invested in another company betting on the same theme. It features in the latter part of this book.

Trigger #6: Low base effect

Suppose there are two grocery retailing companies. Company A has only a single store in a metro city and clocks an annual net profit of Rs 10 crore. Company B has 100 retail stores spread across the country and clocks an annual net profit of Rs 1000 crore. If both companies have a similar operational matrix, which one would you bet on for exponential earnings expansion?

Obviously, the answer would be company A, because just by adding one more store it can double its profits. It would not take more than one year for the company to expand from a single store to ten stores—i.e., theoretically, the company has ten times earnings expansion potential in a single year. However, company B already has 100 stores, and it would take another 1000 new stores for the company to report ten times earnings expansion. And this is not feasible in a single year. Thus, given 'similar operational efficiencies', company A would be the obvious preference for multibagger investing. The keyword is 'similar operational efficiencies'. In the above examples, I have assumed that both companies can earn profits of Rs 10 crore from a single store without stretching the balance sheet. If company A was struggling with its single store then the entire equation would reverse. Suppose, despite years of operation, company A continues to report an annual loss of Rs 10 crore from the single store, then, theoretically, even if it expanded to ten stores, the loss could also multiply by a factor of 10!

Thus, given a choice between a large-cap and a micro-cap stock with similar operational efficiencies, the micro-cap stock can easily multiply wealth for investors. Overall, a well-managed micro-cap company can easily expand profitability and market capitalization on account of its low base effect. However, low base effect alone cannot be an investment rationale for choosing stocks with multibagger potential.

Trigger #7: Broader market strength

Earnings expansion has no correlation with the overall market mood, but PE expansion calls for strength in the overall market. The broader market consists of a large number of shares. In the Indian context, we can consider the NIFTY 500 as a broader index that represents more than 95 per cent of the free-float market capitalization in the country. A rally in the NIFTY 500 index always triggers PE expansion.

Irrespective of whether it is a bull or bear market, a business can keep growing. A restaurant owner can keep increasing the profitability of his business without bull market support. Thus, earnings expansion is not dependent on the overall market condition. With proper analysis, it is relatively easier to predict earnings expansion. Business owners can also predict or offer guidance on earnings expansion. However, PE expansion is difficult to predict because there are a lot of moving variables that trigger a bull or bear market.

Chemcrux Enterprises witnessed a considerable increase in net profit and EPS from 2017 to early 2020. In FY2017, the net profit was Rs 1.5 crore; and in FY2020, it had jumped to Rs 10.6 crore. Despite the ten times jump in net profit and EPS, the stock price appreciated by only 2 times because the overall market was not in a bull phase. It is always difficult for the PE ratio to expand in the absence of a bull market. Thus, despite the ten times jump in earnings recorded by the company, the PE ratio of the stock remained in its earlier zone. However, from April 2020 to early 2022, the overall market witnessed a strong bull run. With this broader market support, the PE ratio of Chemcrux expanded by more than six times, and as a result stock price jumped by more than thirteen times in the same period.

Remember, when a stock witnesses continuous earnings expansion, sooner or later the PE ratio will follow, but the reverse is not true. If the PE ratio keeps moving up in the absence of earnings expansion, then sooner or later the ratio will move in the reverse direction. Here is a summarized table showing stock price movements under different circumstances:

Earnings Expansion	PE Expansion	Stock Price Returns
Yes	Yes	Multibagger returns
Yes	No	Price consolidation, good set-up for multibagger returns in the coming days
No	Yes	Time to book profit, PE expansion can't continue forever without earnings support
No	No	Wealth Destruction

Miscellaneous Triggers

Here are a few additional triggers worth mentioning:

Bigger office: While a company shifts to a bigger office, it is an indication that the stock can reward investors in a big way. Back in 2018, AGM, the chairman of Lancer Container, was very proud of shifting to a bigger office. He offered a guided tour to shareholders around the new office. It increased my conviction manifold. Why would someone invest a few crores in a bigger office unless he had something big in mind? No major improvements in financials were noticed in FY18, FY19 and FY20, but from FY21 onwards, sales and profits jumped manifold as did the stock price. So, the seed sown back in 2018 ultimately bore fruit from 2021 onwards.

Jump in employees: It may not always be possible for an investor to track, whether the company moves to a bigger office or not. However, one can easily track the number of employees. Every listed company needs to mandatorily disclose the number of employees in its annual report. A closer look at the annual report reveals the total number of employees as of 31 March that financial year. If you notice a considerable jump in the total number of employees, then it can indicate something big is coming. Why would a company double or triple manpower unless there is some visibility of multifold business growth? There was a visible jump in the total number of employees in all of my multibagger stocks, such as Chemcrux, Lancer, Can Fin Homes and Caplin Point Lab. Obviously, don't invest in any stock only because of a visible jump in employees, do consider all other parameters discussed above before investing.

SME companies desirous to be in the big league: Companies that are listed in the BSE SME and NSE SME segment are required to disclose only half-yearly financial numbers, not quarterly numbers, unlike companies listed in the mainboard NSE and BSE. Special attention is required for the SME companies that disclose quarterly business updates and hold conference calls with investors despite it not being a mandatory requirement. Such things are an indication that the management truly desires to take their company into the big league of mainboard NSE or BSE. While the company jumps from the SME segment to the mainboard segment, it automatically creates multibagger returns for investors. Companies such as Sirca Paints and Prevest Denpro are examples from my multibagger portfolio that disclosed quarterly updates and arranged conference calls even during the initial days of their SME journey.

3.3 Case Study from My Multibagger Stocks

Before investing in any stock with expectations of multibagger returns, you must be clear about the possible triggers for earnings and PE expansion. For a clear understanding of this, have a look at the triggers that I relied upon before investing in potential multibagger Lancer Container.

Case Study: Lancer Container

Lancer Container is in the business of freight forwarding, clearing, non-vessel operating common carriers (NVOCC) and trading in containers. The prospects of the company are linked to global maritime trade. The stock first grabbed my attention in March 2017. Let's have a look at my initial investment rationale and how the stock turned out to be a multibagger.

Earnings expansion drivers (as of 2017)

*   **Huge opportunity size**: The freight forwarding and container trading segment is crowded with a lot of small, unorganized regional players. Lancer Container too was a small player, with FY2017 total sales of Rs 78 crore and net profit of only Rs 2 crore. However, at every AGM, the management communicated that it was firm in its resolve to achieve its target of Rs 1000 crore in sales within the next five to six years. Given the nature of easily scalable businesses in a fragmented industry, it was

not a tall claim. I initiated my position, thinking that even if the management could achieve 50 per cent of the targeted sales, then huge wealth creation would result.

- **Energetic, growth-hungry management**: The chairman and founder of the company, Abdul Khalik Chaitaiwala, had lofty visions. I met with him twice, at the 2017 and 2018 AGMs, and every time I was impressed with his vision. Most importantly, management always walked the talk, and the company's financial performance never deviated greatly from the guidance.
- **Low base effect**: Given the FY2017 sales figure of Rs 78 crore and net profit of Rs 2 crore, the earnings expansion that was talked about was never a tall claim.

PE expansion drivers (as of 2017)

- **Asset-light business model**: Container manufacturing is an asset-heavy business. However, the company didn't opt to manufacture containers; rather, as per the supply-demand scenario, it preferred to take a few containers on lease and own another few. Thus, the business maintained an asset-light model, which was evident from its high asset-turnover ratio (compared with its peers) and low debt-to-equity ratio.
- **Margin expansion**: Back in March 2017, the company had 3500 containers. Its target was to double the number of containers within the next two years, which meant the economies of scale would come into play, paving the way for margin expansion.
- **Less discovered stock**: Being a BSE-SME-listed company of around Rs 20 crore in market capitalization (as of 2017), the stock was off the radar of analysts, brokerage

houses, etc. I was sure that over the next four to five years, even if the management reached only the halfway mark of its target of Rs 1000 crore in revenue, then too the stock would grab the attention of the wider market, and would command a higher price-to-earnings multiple.

How the story played out

(Stock price and EPS in the following section are as per June 2022 data; if the stock undergoes a split or there is a bonus issue after this date, then this data will have to be adjusted accordingly.)

The business continued to grow as per the management guidance. In keeping with the sales trajectory (Fig. 3.4), revenue jumped by 41 per cent in FY2018, by 80 per cent in FY2019 and then by 34 per cent in FY2020. From Rs 79.34 crore in FY2017, revenue jumped by more than three times by the end of FY2020. Now, let's have a look at how much all this aided the stock price movement.

Total Revenue Annual Cr of Lancer Container Lines Ltd.

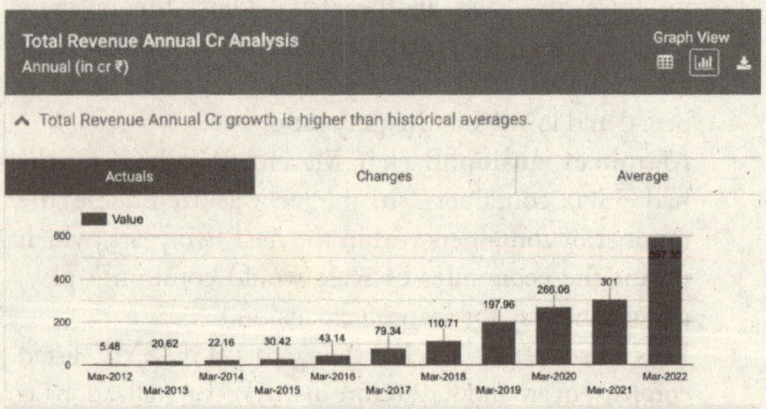

Fig. 3.4: Lancer Container, annual revenue trajectory

Despite healthy revenue growth and container addition, the stock price disappointed in 2018 and 2019. From January 2018 to December 2019, the stock price declined by more than 60 per cent. The weakness continued in the first half of 2020 too. In fact, if you consider the period between March 2017 and March 2020, you will find that despite revenue growing by more than three times, the stock price remained in a narrow zone.

Fig. 3.5: Stock price chart of Lancer Container

The catch is in the margin

Despite healthy revenue growth, erratic margins restricted profit growth and, as a result, the weakness in the stock price continued in 2020. A clear picture will emerge if you look at the margin trajectory.

The margin trajectory suggests that the company struggled to maintain similar profitability during the FY2018–FY2020 period. The 60 per cent decline in the stock price that we noticed from January 2018 to December 2019 can be attributed to the fall in the company's profit margin, from 6.25 per cent in FY2018 to 3.02 per cent in FY2020. This once again establishes the fact that improvement in margin is a must for PE expansion; and without PE expansion the stock price suffers.

Net Profit Margin Annual % of Lancer Container Lines Ltd.

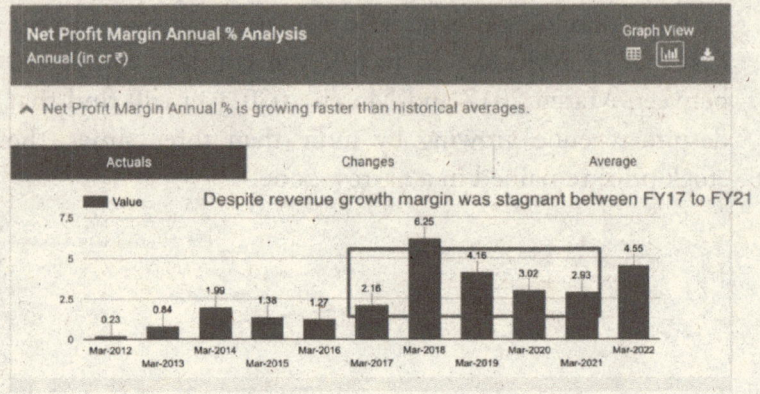

Fig. 3.6: Lancer Container, Margin Trajectory

In the context of the 60 per cent price decline in stock price over the 2018–20 period, you might ask questions, such as:

1. Why did you continue holding on to the stock despite such a sharp price decline?
2. Don't you believe in the stop-loss concept?
3. How did you develop the conviction to hold on to the shares, or was it just that luck favoured you in this matter?

I will address all these questions in the latter part of this book. So far, I hope the importance of margin growth to stock price movement is clear.

'Irrespective of sales growth, if net profit margin declines then the stock price will disappoint.'

Post the COVID-19 lockdowns (2021 onwards)

The business got a sudden boost after the pandemic-related lockdowns. A statement from the company management said:

'With the impact of Covid-19 pandemic and resulting lockdowns on the downfall, the Shipping industry has received a boost in the demand for containers. The increasing freight charges globally and congestion at Chinese Ports have presented an optimistic outlook for the Indian Container Shipping business. In tune with this outlook, Lancer Container Lines has reported the highest ever business performance for the second quarter ended 30th September 2021. We have been able to increase our PAT margins to 4.39% in Q2FY22 as compared to 2.68% Q1FY22. Our Revenue from operations stands at 1369.19 Mn till end of September, 2021 reporting a growth of 87% vis-à-vis H1 FY 21. This is mainly supported by our NVOCC business that witnessed sustained growth due to healthy demand for FCL & LCL shipments which led an expansion of our market share. We have also brought down our debt substantially in FY22, primarily on account of a sharp increase in profitability and improved cash accruals. However, we believe our EBIDTA margins will improve further on account of increased revenue from various business segments and healthy cost management.'

With these great financial numbers, the management issued an even better business outlook. The expectation was 80 per cent revenue growth for FY2022, with margin improvement.

Net Profit Annual Cr of Lancer Container Lines Ltd.

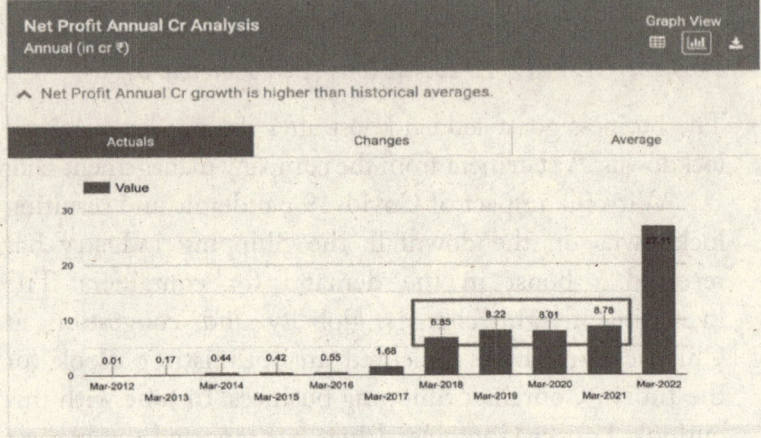

Fig. 3.7: Annual profit trajectory of Lancer Container

The total revenue, EBITDA margin and net profit figures ballooned in FY2022 (April 2021 to March 2022). The stock price also reacted accordingly, jumping more than ten times in FY22 alone!

Here is the summarized version of my multibagger journey with Lancer Container:

1. I had initiated the investment in Lancer Container in March 2017 hoping for multibagger returns, keeping in mind the huge opportunity size, growth-hungry management, low base effect, asset-light business model and high margin expansion probability that would pave way for earnings and PE expansion.

2. Despite healthy revenue growth, the stock price moved nowhere from March 2017 to July 2020, over more than three years, because of profit margin contraction.

3. I had expectations of a four-to-five times return on investment by 2021 or 2022. However, the COVID-related lockdowns triggered a global container shortage that increased freight rates manifold. This industry tailwind helped the company report a three-time jump in earnings in FY2022. Along with margin expansion, PE ratio expansion of more than five times paved the way for an increase of more than ten times in the stock price.

4. Sensing that the industry tailwind would not remain forever, I started booking profits on the stock in September 2021. By January 2022, I sold all my holdings in it, obtaining an overall return of nine times on my investment. Interestingly, after my exit, the stock price further doubled. Does that mean my exit decision was wrong? Not really, because at some stage, profit booking is required to utilize the fund for fulfilling dreams like buying a car or a house or something expensive or maybe funding a foreign tour. If the company has strength, then the stock price can't stop appreciating just because someone made an exit! So, as long as you made some profit, there's no point in repenting regarding stock price appreciation after the exit.

The key decision that helped me earn a nine-time return on investment was to hold Lancer Container over the 2018–20 period when the stock price tanked by around 60 per cent from its peak levels. It is always difficult to hold one's nerve after a 50–60 per cent fall in investment value. At that stage, you need to determine whether the stock has the potential to bounce back or if it will continue sliding. Back in 2018–20, MRSS, Focus Suites and Lancer—all three of my portfolio stocks—were down by around 60 per cent. I booked a huge loss in MRSS and Focus Suites but kept on holding Lancer Container. In the coming years, MRSS and Focus continued their downward journey, the stock price dropped by around 90–95 per cent from the 2017 level while Lancer bounced back and turned multibagger.

Thus, more than stock selection, the rational decision-making ability while the stock price tanks determines success in a multibagger's journey. You need to remember that the stock price of the world's best company can suffer a setback just because of external market conditions. Sometimes, the stock price comes under pressure due to company-specific internal reasons and sometimes for external reasons. Moreover, the magnitude of company-specific internal reasons also varies; a few companies can make a swift comeback and a few can't. It is always a difficult task to determine whether the company can make a swift comeback or not. Reading books or study materials will not suffice; a few years of experience and studying the maximum possible number of case studies can help in such a critical decision-making process. On my website, www.prasenjitpaul.com, under a multibagger subscription, I keep sharing updates and my buy/sell rationale on potential multibagger stocks. The subscription will help you to properly navigate your multibagger journey; do check it out.

'In the journey of multibaggers, at some point, a few of your portfolio shares will show a 40–60 per cent drawdown from your purchase price. At such a junction, a rational decision-making ability determines success in the multibagger journey.'

Chapter 4

How to Avoid Wealth Destroyers

4.1 Introduction

So far, we have used the term 'multibagger' quite often. Let me introduce another term— 'multibeggar'. There is very little difference in the spelling of these two terms, so much so that if you are reading fast you may not spot the difference! Well, the term 'multibeggar' is a combination of two words—'multi' and 'beggar'—and means the exact opposite of 'multibagger'. As we know, a beggar is someone who is poor and begs for money or food. So, the term 'multibeggar' can be used for stocks that make the investor poorer; they are, in more direct terms, wealth destroyers.

We know that the small-cap and micro-cap space is great for multibagger hunting. However, the fact remains that more than 90 per cent of small-cap and micro cap stocks destroy wealth over the long run. So, random investment in a basket of lesser-known micro-cap stocks can lead to an immense loss in your overall portfolio. You can prevent this only if you have a clear idea of what not to do. The Internet is filled with multibagger stock tips. Search for 'multibagger stocks' on YouTube, Twitter, Telegram, etc., and you will find hundreds of results. Instead of following multibagger tips, a comprehensive guide on what to avoid can prove highly beneficial to you because the majority of micro-cap companies turn out to be multibeggars or wealth destroyers.

In this chapter, I will first write about the stocks that turned my investments sour, along with case studies and my learnings, and then give you comprehensive guidance on what to avoid.

4.2 Wealth Destroyers in My Investment Career

The wealth destroyers in my investment career probably far outnumber the multibaggers. You might then ask that, if this was the case, how did my portfolio generate more than 100 times the returns over the last decade? Well, it's simple. The maximum loss is limited to well below the 100 per cent mark, but there is no upside limit when it comes to profits from multibaggers. While a stock generates a nine-time return on investment, it translates into a profit of 800 per cent. A single instance of this quantum of returns, as Lancer Container delivered for me, can make up for all the losses in one's portfolio.

From 2017 to 2022, while Chemcrux Enterprises and Lancer Container turned notable multibaggers in my portfolio, stocks like MRSS, Focus Suites, Sarveshwar Foods, Global Education, Jhandewalas Foods, Sysco Industries, Shanti Overseas, Dr Lalchandani Lab,

Mandhana Industries and Sintex Industries proved to be wealth destroyers. I lost money from multiple mid-caps and large-caps as well, but I am excluding those from this book because there was no expectation of multibagger returns from those stocks. In the current context, we'll study another portfolio stock of mine, Sarveshwar Foods, to understand my investment rationale and what went wrong.

Case Study #1: Sarveshwar Foods

Based out of Jammu, Sarveshwar Foods is engaged in the processing and marketing of branded and unbranded basmati and non-basmati rice in the domestic and international markets. Basmati, long-grained and fine in texture, is one of the most popular rice varieties in the world. The company is involved in procurement, storage, milling, sorting, packaging, branding and distribution of rice, and thus has a presence in the entire rice value chain. Its product portfolio consists of basmati and non-basmati rice of various kinds, including white raw rice, steamed rice, broken rice, brown rice and parboiled rice.

The company grabbed my attention at the time of its IPO (in the NSE SME segment) in March 2018. Let's have a quick look at my investment rationale for this at the time:

1. The company shared an ambitious target for its organic range of food products under the brand name 'Nimbark'.
2. Organic food was the talk of the town, and it fetches higher margins, so any company that can successfully

penetrate the organic food segment must experience margin expansion, which is an essential trigger for multibagger returns.

3. On 17 May 2018, the company launched its flagship retail store named 'Nimbark: Living the Satvik Way' for organic products at Channi Himmat in Jammu.

4. The company had planned to open many more Nimbark stores for selling its organic range of food products like red rice, brown rice, pulses, dried fruit, spices, breakfast cereals, edible oils, etc.

5. The Nimbark range of products was also listed on e-commerce websites like Amazon, Flipkart, etc.

6. Until March 2018, the company registered consistent growth. Net profit, which amounted to Rs 5.48 crore in FY2016, jumped by around three times, to Rs 16.53 crore in FY2018.

7. Average return on equity was more than 25 per cent.

8. The negative was the comparatively higher debt in its books and the higher cash conversion cycle. I thought the IPO money would help it pare down the debt and that, going forward, the high-margin Nimbark product range would help strengthen the balance sheet further.

9. The IPO was priced at a PE ratio of only 13. Thus, I was under the impression that if the organic food range elevated the overall margin of the business, then the PE ratio could reasonably expand into the 20–22 range, paving way for multibagger returns from the stock.

Overall, as per the vision of the management to promote organic food products, I got the impression that, going forward, earnings could expand by 50–60 per cent over the next two to three years and the PE ratio could also expand from that 13-odd level to the 20–22 range; and if both these happened, then the stock price could double from the IPO price. Thus, I had invested at the IPO price of Rs 85 and then added a few more quantities at around Rs 70–72.

Since the IPO listing, the stock price never touched the Rs 85 level. Afterwards, in 2018, the small-cap index experienced a big crash and liquidity in the SME segment dried up, diminishing the chances of the stock price rebounding. I sold my entire investment in 2018 itself, in the Rs 45–50 range, and ended up with a loss of around 40 per cent on my investment. My decision proved correct because the stock price continued its downward journey for the next three years until 2021. At one point, the price crashed to the Rs 8–10 level, which was an 88 per cent drawdown from the IPO price. At the time of writing this book, the stock price had rebounded and was again hovering at the Rs 45–50 level.

What went wrong with Sarveshwar Foods?

1. The Nimbark stores didn't do well, as per the management's plan. It looks as though the entire product range was not well accepted by the consumer. At the time of writing this book, I was checking the product reviews on Amazon and noticed that sales were muted and there was negative customer feedback.
2. Without enough contribution from the organic food range, the company has little pricing power and remains dependent on traditional basmati rice sales. In 2018–19, the entire basmati rice market faced headwinds.

3. The most important reason for wealth destruction in this case was profit-margin contraction. We are now well aware of the fact that in the absence of margin expansion, both earnings and PE ratio contract, making way for a 'multibeggar' journey.

4. The company has recently reported a jump in overall sales. Total revenue amounted to Rs 481 crore in FY2018, and that jumped to Rs 605 crore in FY2022, but during the same period, the net profit margin reduced from 3.43 per cent to only 0.52 per cent. This margin slump ensured the exact reverse journey of a multibagger for the stock.

5. Total debt increased further and the cash conversion cycle was further stretched, making it difficult for the stock price to rebound.

Lessons to learn

1. Total sales or revenue growth is the least important parameter in the multibagger journey. It has been noted frequently that despite a significant jump in total revenue, a company's stock price has continued its downward journey.

2. Margin expansion is the most important trigger for multibagger returns. Expanded margins not only push earnings growth but also help in PE expansion, paving the way for multibagger returns.

3. Debt will remain the most dangerous four-letter word in investing. Incremental debt can completely change the business prospects of a company.

4. Irrespective of the management's commentary about the bright prospects for their company, it is always

better to avoid companies with increasing debt and lengthening cash conversion cycles.

Case Study #2

In the case of another wealth destroyer in my portfolio, I strongly believe a company floated an IPO only to steal money from investors. It was a sophisticated, well-executed 'daylight robbery', though no investigating agency can prove it to be one. I don't want to name the company as I will then be inviting legal action against myself as I too cannot prove that the IPO was a massive theft. The purpose of this book is to help you earn multibagger returns from stocks and not to invite unnecessary controversy.

The company claimed it catered to the high-growth segment of FMCG and pharma players with specialized packaging materials. They were in the early growth stage and had reported profit growth of over 40 per cent in a few years. The company raised Rs 2.17 crore from its IPO, and after listing, the stock performed well for the next two years. The company continued its growth journey and began to talk about capacity expansion. As long as the stock price was moving well, no one had any idea what was brewing in the minds of the promoters. After two years of the listing, all of a sudden, the company disclosed to the stock exchange that there was a massive accidental fire in its factory that damaged almost all of its inventory and machinery. In genuine fire accidents, the company raises claims with its insurance company. Surprisingly, the company mentioned that the factory was not insured at all, which is hard to believe because they had borrowings from State Bank of

India (SBI), and banks check insurance papers before loan disbursal. Moreover, a genuine business always opts for factory insurance. My rough guess is that the fire incident was projected only to cover up the fictitious profits of the company over the last few years. At a single stroke, they could now clear the balance sheet, and whatever reserves were accumulated could be reversed in a single quarter. After disclosing the fire incident, the stock hit the lower circuits consecutively over the next few trading days. This meant that even if you desired to sell the stock you could not, as there was no buyer, liquidity having dried up completely. By the time some buyers emerged, breaking the lower circuit for the stock, its price had already crashed by around 60 per cent from its recent peak. I was able to exit with an overall loss of about 50 per cent on my investment.

A few months later, SBI declared their loan to the company as an NPA. The stock price continued its downward journey. Interestingly, the company failed to publish its financial results, citing the reason that all its important documents were burnt in the fire! Within a few months, the stock turned into a penny stock, destroying more than 95 per cent of investor wealth. BSE then delisted it for reasons of non-compliance. Overall, the entire amount of Rs 2.17 crore that the company had collected from various investors in the IPO was reduced to zero. The funds were never used for business purposes. Rather, the promoters, the merchant bankers and whoever else was involved in the IPO utilized the funds for their own enjoyment. The entire Rs 2.17 crore is gone forever.

In another bizarre incident reported by moneycontrol. com, another SME company accused its merchant bankers of siphoning off its IPO funds![1] Trekkingtoes.com, a Jaipur-based new-age digital start-up involved in intercity cab rental services, raised Rs 4.54 crore from its IPO in August 2020. The company registered a complaint with SEBI saying it had no knowledge of the capital markets and that an advisory company had suggested to them that instead of borrowing funds, they could raise money from the public via an IPO. The same advisory firm later siphoned off around Rs 4 crore from the IPO, leaving the company with only Rs 40–50 lakh from the public issue. I don't know whether any progress in the investigation has been made. Overall, the stock price crashed by more than 80 per cent, destroying investor wealth entirely.

Such stories are common with micro-cap stocks, and most of them go unreported by media houses. You will often find media headlines saying a particular stock generated ten times or twenty times returns. However, every few years, the stock price of a few hundred companies crashes by more than 90 per cent, and many of them are delisted. Have you noticed any dedicated segment in any financial newspaper or website covering these wealth destroyers?

'A very large number of stocks are delisted from the stock exchange after they have caused massive wealth destruction, and this is not reported by the media, leaving many market participants unaware of such incidents.'

You can never know what is going on inside the mind of promoters. There are numerous instances of companies raising funds via IPOs on the SME platform with the sole intention of stealing public money. There are strict regulations for a company issuing an IPO on mainboard BSE or NSE, but the regulations are much more relaxed for the SME segment to encourage start-ups and smaller firms. Unfortunately, many promoters, merchant bankers and investor relations companies misuse the platform. For investors, it is always difficult to guess the actual intention of promoters. That is why, regardless of the detailed research you might have done, many micro-cap stocks turn out to be wealth destroyers. Proper exit timing and diversification in multiple bets are a must to minimize the damage dealt to your portfolio on account of this.

> 'Most of the micro-cap stocks are just trash; less than 1 per cent of them generate massive wealth for investors. Thus, irrespective of your expertise and research, you must face loss in some instances of micro-cap investment. Only proper diversification and exit timing can preserve the overall portfolio.'

4.3 Checklist for Spotting Wealth Destroyers

Difficult-to-understand business

If, despite elaborate research and effort on your part, you can't understand the exact business of the company or what exactly it does, then it is better to give it a miss. Kindly note that I am not talking in the context of 'area of competence'. I'm not saying that if you are a civil engineer, then you are competent to concentrate on stocks of real estate, building materials and allied companies, because it can happen that these particular sectors go into a structural downtrend at the same time over the long run, in which case multibaggers cannot emerge from this particular segment. Similarly, for a bank employee, it might be easier to understand banking stocks, but he should focus beyond banking in his quest for multibagger returns. Interestingly, during my college years, chemistry was my least preferred subject, but most of my multibagger stocks were from the chemicals and pharma industries.

Here, 'difficult-to-understand' refers to companies whose primary business operation remains opaque to most market participants. Take the example of Majestic Research Services and Solutions (MRSS) and another group company, Focus Suites Solutions and Services, both market research agencies catering to international as well as domestic clients. I had invested in both, in view of their excellent growth, optimistic management commentary, minimal debt, strong return on equity (ROE) and return on capital employed (ROCE). However, even after elaborate research and analysis on my part, it was not clear exactly what kind of market research the company did. In fact, when I attended its AGM back in September 2018, the majority of the shareholders raised the same question to the management, 'What is the exact nature of the business?' This clearly indicated that I was not the only one who had this question to ask the company. After the AGM, I completely exited from the stock, but the damage was already done; I lost around 70 per cent of my investment in the two stocks.

Many service-related businesses in the micro-cap and small-cap space are difficult to understand in view of the nature of their operations. When it comes to the manufacturing segment, e.g., pharma, chemicals, food processing, building materials and the automotive industry, we can obtain a clear idea of the product range, total capacity, capacity expansion plans (if any), factory location, etc. We can even visit the company factory to exactly understand the business. With some effort, anyone can understand such businesses. Even within the service segment, businesses that cater to logistics, financial needs, etc., are easy to understand, but those that are in information technology, market research, consultancy, etc., are the most difficult to understand. The problem is not so bad when it comes to large-cap and mid-cap companies. We all come to know about the nature of their business, the location of their offices nationwide and their clients (such as those of TCS, Infosys, Wipro, L&T Infotech, etc.), but if an unknown company claims that it is in the business of new-tech or automation, it becomes very hard to verify this. One of my other investments that comes to mind is Global Education. Although I didn't lose money from that investment, I sold the stock, as even after visiting their offices, I was not convinced about the nature of their business. It is equally true that many lesser-known micro-cap IT shares have made it big, but the number of wealth destroyers is far higher than the number of multibaggers in this segment. The rule that you can follow here is that if you are not fully convinced about the nature of the company's business, even after visiting their office and interacting with the management, then it is better to overlook the stock.

'While hunting for multibaggers in the small-cap and micro-cap space, to be on the safe side, it is better to avoid difficult-to-understand businesses.'

Margin contraction

In chapter 3, we elaborated on the importance of margin expansion in a stock's multibagger journey. In fact, profit margin expansion is perhaps the most important factor in multibagger returns. Naturally, margin contraction is the biggest contributor to wealth destruction. Let's have a look at the net profit margin trend of Nandan Denim over a ten-year period.

Net Profit Margin Annual % of Nandan Denim Ltd.

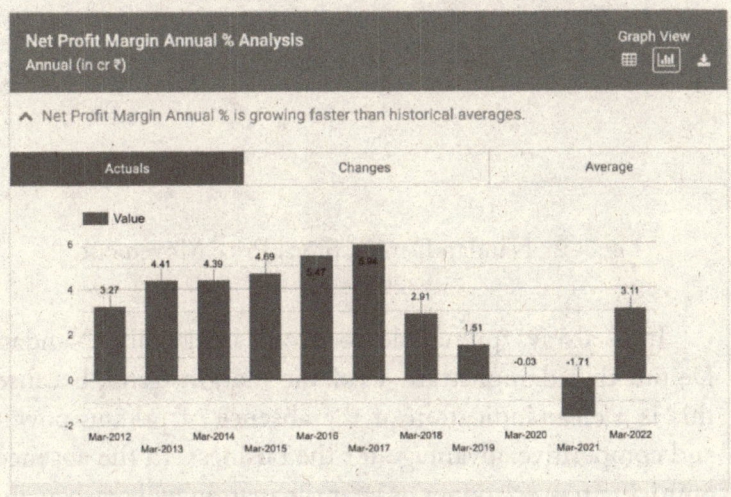

Fig. 4.1: Nandan Denim, Net Profit Margin Trend, 2012–22

As is clear from Fig. 4.1, net profit margin was range-bound, showing an improving trend from FY2012 to FY2017. However, from calendar year 2017 itself, the margin started to deteriorate and moved into negative territory in FY2021. A negative profit margin denotes net loss in that financial year. If you look at the stock price movement of Nandan Denim in Fig. 4.2, you will find that the stock performed well from 2013 to 2017. However, it crashed by more than 80 per cent in the 2018–20 period. Later, in FY2022, its margin rose and the stock price also witnessed a significant jump.

Fig. 4.2: Nandan Denim, Stock Price Movement,
2015–22

It is always preferable to avoid stocks like Nandan Denim that demonstrate a volatile margin trend, because this is a clear indication of the absence of pricing power and competitive advantage for the business. In the absence of pricing power, sooner or later the margin will crash again and so will the stock price.

'To be on the safe side while hunting for multibaggers in the small-cap and micro-cap space, it is better to avoid companies that have historically demonstrated a highly volatile margin trend.'

Promoters holding less than 50 per cent

Every listed company is required to disclose its shareholding pattern. You will find the detailed shareholding pattern of any company on the websites of the stock exchanges (NSE or BSE) on which it is listed. Shareholders are classified into two groups:

1. **Promoters and promoter group**: Promoters are the owners of the business. They can be either domestic or foreign entities, or a group of individuals. Relatives of promoters owning shares also fall under the promoter group.
2. **Public group**: This group consists of shareholders other than promoters, and their holdings would be listed under 'public shareholding'. Foreign institutional investors, domestic institutional investors, banks, money managers, mutual funds, insurance companies, individuals, etc., come under this group.

No one knows a company better than its owners. Thus, a lower percentage of promoter holding in companies indicates lower promoter confidence in the business; but this can also result from excessive equity dilution by the promoters. I had noticed promoter shareholding of more than 50 per cent among all the small-cap and micro-cap stocks that generated multibagger returns for me. Remember, I am talking only about the small-cap and micro-cap segment. There are many large cap and mid-cap companies where promoter shareholding is zero, but score very high in corporate governance and return on investment. Well-known large-cap and mid-cap shares like ICICI Bank, Larsen & Toubro, ITC, City Union Bank, BSE and Indian Energy Exchange have zero promoter shareholding, but that doesn't necessarily mean that they are a bad choice for investment. Zero promoter holding indicates a professionally managed company not influenced by any particular founding family (promoter). Mostly, such companies are promoted by multiple large institutions that appoint professionals to manage their day-to-day activities.

However, when it comes to the small-cap and micro-cap space, and when the company is still in an early growth stage, then the higher the promoter holding, the better it is for the minority shareholders. Regulations have capped the promoter holding in a listed stock at 75 per cent. Promoter holding anywhere between 60 and 75 per cent adds extra confidence to the investor. Obviously, promoter shareholding should not be the only investment criterion; it should be considered along with other parameters.

> *To be on the safe side while hunting for multibaggers in the small-cap and micro-cap space, avoid companies with promoter shareholding of less than 50 per cent.'*

Decreasing promoter stake

Promoters can reduce their stake in their companies for various reasons. This can have different implications for different stocks. For large-cap and mid-cap stocks, we can't conclude anything by merely looking at the decreasing promoter stake. Sometimes, just like you and me, promoters, too, book partial profits on their investment.

In fact, they have the right to enjoy business profits. It's not necessarily a bad thing if they sell a part of their stake. They are in the business of earning money, and they have been working for it for fifteen to twenty years, some for over fifty years too! For example, the promoters of Page Industries were reducing their stake during 2012–15; still, the stock price appreciated by more than 200 per cent during the same period. Moreover, promoters of banking and financial companies often dilute their stakes to raise funds, which is generally a positive action. We can consider money as raw material when it comes to the banking business. The more money the business can have, the more it can lend (offer loans) and thus make more profits. So, for banking stocks, it is not always a bad thing. However, for small-cap and micro-cap stocks, where the business is still in the early stage and has a lot of growth potential going ahead, stake sales by promoters should be taken as a cautionary note.

For a mature business like a large-cap or mid-cap company, stake sales by promoters can indicate something completely different, but for a small-cap or micro-cap company where there is a lot of growth visibility ahead, a reduction in promoter stake is not a good sign. I have been tracking a micro-cap stock, Valiant Organics, since 2019–20. The company had very optimistic capacity expansion plans with bright prospects. The operating profit margin was consistent, at around 30 per cent. Average ROE and ROCE were around 30 per cent and the company's debt-to-equity ratio was less than 0.4. There was nothing to complain about. I had almost made up my mind to invest in the stock but noticed one drawback; the promoters kept reducing their stake. It was really surprising to note that on one hand, the promoters were sharing optimistic guidance, talking about their capacity expansion plans and predicting a lot of growth ahead, while on other hand, they themselves were reducing ownership on a consistent basis. Here is the promoter holding in Valiant Organics from 2019 to 2022:

Historical shareholding details of Promoter in Valiant Organics Ltd. (VALIANTORG)   ×

QUARTER	NAME	TOTAL NO. SHARES HELD	PERCENT HOLDING	PLEDGED	
				SHARES	%
Mar 2022	Total	10,591,143	39.00%	25,021	0.24%
Dec 2021	Total	10,591,468	39.01%	25,021	0.24%
Sep 2021	Total	11,013,577	40.56%	25,085	0.23%
Jun 2021	Total	11,309,652	41.65%	25,015	0.22%
Mar 2021	Total	11,582,724	42.66%	0	0.00%
Jan 13, 2021	Total	11,633,154	42.84%	0	0.00%
Dec 2020	Total	11,633,154	42.84%	0	0.00%
Nov 04, 2020	Total	5,867,440	43.22%	0	0.00%
Nov 04, 2020	Total	5,867,440	43.22%	0	0.00%
Sep 2020	Total	5,155,158	42.43%	0	0.00%
Mar 2020	Total	5,803,408	47.77%	0	0.00%
Sep 2019	Total	5,803,408	47.77%	0	0.00%

Fig. 4.3: Valiant Organics, Promoter Shareholding, 2019–22

Common sense suggests that, if a business owner senses a bright future with strong growth for his company, he should never reduce his ownership of it. In the case of Valiant

Organics, promoter shareholding reduced from 47.77 per cent in March 2020 to 42.84 per cent in December 2020. Because of this single negative, I didn't invest in the stock. The strategy paid off. Although the stock appreciated throughout 2020, over 2021 and 2022, it crashed by more than 66 per cent from its 2020 peak. Further, its financial performance deteriorated in FY2022, with a significant drop in margin and profitability, proving my fears correct.

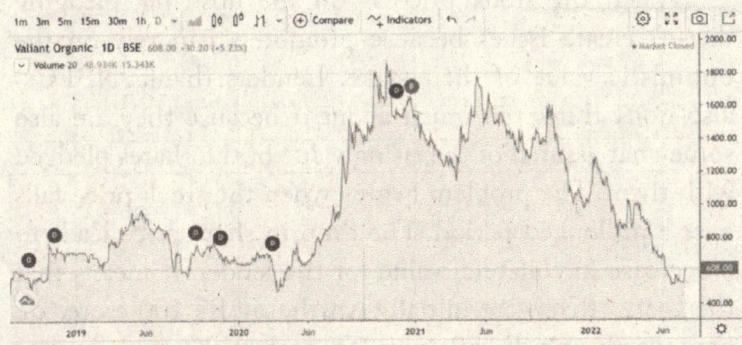

Fig. 4.4: Valiant Organics, Stock Price Chart

Overall, although the reduction of promoter stake in large-caps and mid-caps can be a mixed bag, when it comes to small-caps and micro-caps, it is always better to see it as a negative.

'While hunting for multibaggers in the small-cap and micro-cap space, to be on the safe side, avoid companies where promoters are reducing their stake.'

Pledged shareholding

Shares are considered assets, and hence, banks consider them as security against which they can offer loans. Promoters often pledge their shares as collateral for fundraising—this is the last option for them to raise funds. It means that no one else is ready to provide them with a loan because either the company's prospects are not bright, or the company has high debt and might be under financial constraints (and pledging shares is the only option left).

When the stock price is on the upswing, pledging doesn't create issues because promoters can rely on the optimistic value of their stake. Lenders (banks/NBFCs) also don't think too much about it because they are also somewhat assured of the rising value of the shares pledged with them. The problem begins when the stock price falls over a prolonged period. The drop in share price leads to a decrease in collateral value for the lender. It means that the shares that were initially worth, say Rs 100 crore, are now worth only Rs 50 crore. To protect the loan amount and limit the risk, the lender asks for more collateral and promoters are forced to pledge more of their shares. If they don't do this, the lender has the right to sell the pledged shares in the market and recover the loan. Whenever lenders begin to offload pledged shares in the open market, a huge price decline in the stock follows. There are many well-known companies (like Zee Enterprise, Fortis, etc.) that plunged into trouble following the pledging of their shares by the promoters. Companies with a high quantum of pledged promoter-owned shares can experience a sharp drop in their stock price at any point.

When it comes to large-cap and mid-cap stocks, one can still ignore it if the pledged shares constitute a very small percentage or if their quantum reduces over a period of time. However, for small-cap or micro-cap stocks, pledged shares can be a red signal, whatever the proportion pledged. Interestingly, if you follow the shareholding pattern in Valiant Organics in Fig. 4.4, you will find that the promoters started pledging their shares from June 2021 onwards. Although the pledge percentage is very small, this single reason is enough to avoid the stock.

'While hunting for multibaggers in the small-cap and micro-cap space, to be on the safe side, it is always better to avoid companies whose promoters have pledged their shares.'

Social media noise

Nowadays you will find plenty of free multibagger stock tips across YouTube, Twitter, Telegram, Facebook and other social media platforms. First, you need to understand that no one in this world is working hard to make you rich free of cost. In your daily lives, do you ever come across any person who is selflessly eager to make you rich? Without commission income, no insurance agent would care about your family's insurance protection. Banks are offering fixed deposits that grow your wealth so that they can lend that money to make profits. From banks to insurance agents and anyone else in the financial ecosystem, everyone is offering their services only because they can earn in the process. If this is so, then why would someone offer you multibagger stock tips free of cost on social media platforms such as Twitter, Telegram or YouTube? The truth is, anyone who is offering tips on stocks with multibagger potential on social sites is doing so with some intention. It is not that every one of them has bad intentions. Some are well-intentioned too. Let's explore the facts.

Paid sponsorship

I have two YouTube channels where I discuss the stock market, mutual funds and personal finance. The first one, named 'Prasenjit Paul', has videos in English and Hindi, and the second channel, 'Prasenjit Paul (Bengali Videos)' caters to an audience that prefers to hear me speak in Bengali. Both channels have a sizeable audience, and as a result, I keep receiving multiple emails such as these:

> *We are an investor relations company working with multiple small-cap companies. Kindly share your commercials for a dedicated video to promote a stock.*
>
> *or*
>
> *Kindly share your pricing to promote an upcoming SME IPO.*

I am not the only one receiving such emails on a frequent basis; whoever has a strong subscriber base on YouTube receives such emails quite often. YouTubers earn anywhere between Rs 10,000 and Rs 80,000 from each of their videos that promote these shady companies. For promoting on Twitter, Facebook and some other platforms, the amount offered is a little less, but the amount can still be anywhere between Rs 5000 and Rs 50,000. You won't find any such video on my YouTube channel. In fact, I prefer to comment only on those micro-cap stocks in which I have a personal holding.

Remember, YouTube is filled with sponsored videos that cover shady, little-known stocks without marking them as 'paid promotion'. Often, such stocks witness sharp spurts in price due to such coverage, paving the way for operators to exit at a good profit, following which the stocks witness a crash. After a few months, these videos are deleted from the platform altogether. As the stock price witnesses a sharp jump following such videos, a few amateur retail investors continue to buy while, on the other side, operators exit at a higher price. After a few months, many retail investors get stuck and face massive losses. Well, it is not that every social media influencer indulges in this practice. There is a lot of good content available across social media sites too, but for a newcomer, it is difficult to separate the wheat from the chaff.

Good intentions—knowledge sharing

Obviously, there are many renowned investors sharing their wisdom on Twitter, and there are indeed some great videos that help you acquire knowledge of the stock market. However, when a particular small-cap or micro-cap share receives undue attention, then it mostly disappoints. We have already learnt that PE expansion is one of the most important factors for multibagger returns. Now, when a stock receives massive attention on social media websites, then we can safely assume that it is well-discovered and is known to a large number of market participants. The price has been fully discovered by then, leaving almost no room for PE expansion; rather, possibilities of PE contraction. In such cases, even if the company continues its earnings expansion, the stock price can remain under pressure on account of PE ratio contraction.

Back in 2020–21, I noticed a gentleman on Twitter continually sharing his bullish view on stocks like Laurus, Solara, Neuland Labs and many others that are mainly in the pharmaceutical segment. Most of these stocks appreciated during the post-COVID lockdown period. With the stock price appreciating, this gentleman's follower count witnessed a massive jump, crossing the 1,00,000 figure. It was apparent that he had no bad intentions but was rather utilizing Twitter as a good knowledge-sharing platform. Now, here comes the interesting part: Although those stocks appreciated a lot in 2020, they began to register massive declines from the second half of 2021. Stocks like Solara and Neuland crashed by more than 60 per cent from their 2021 peaks. Many investors who had put money in these stocks in 2021 were stuck at the top level and unleashed their frustration on Twitter. With his recommended stocks now falling, the trolling and mocking of this gentleman kept increasing. So much so that the gentleman blocked many people who tried to reply to his tweets. My rough guess suggests that he was forced to block many of his followers who blindly invested following his tweets. Now, let's understand what actually changed in those two years. A quick overview suggests that as those stocks received a lot of attention across Twitter, YouTube, etc., their PE ratios expanded a lot during 2020. Most of these stocks experienced more than a 100 per cent increase in their PE ratios. After such huge PE expansion, these companies' operating profit margin came under pressure and that accelerated PE contraction.

Overall, platforms like Twitter, YouTube, etc., are great platforms from which you can gain multiple insights into the market, but they are the worst place to seek multibagger potential stocks. Always remember, the more a stock becomes the talk of the town, the greater the probability of exponential PE decline. And without PE expansion, the stock will disappoint investors.

'Social media platforms like Twitter, YouTube, Telegram, etc. are a great place for learning but a dangerous place to seek multibagger stock tips.'

Chapter 5

How Long to Hold, and When to Sell

5.1 When to Average and When Not To

After a few months of thorough research, Mohit zeroed in on a potential multibagger stock and invested Rs 100 in it. After, say, six months, the following can happen:

1. The stock price drops to Rs 70, and Mohit regrets buying the share at a higher price.
2. The stock price moves up to Rs 150, and Mohit regrets NOT buying more stocks at Rs 100.
3. The stock price remains static and hovers at around Rs 100; Mohit regrets not having done a proper analysis!

Surprisingly, whatever the outcome, regret is a constant. Now, how can one avoid this kind of regret? The first and foremost point that you must keep in mind is that **no matter**

what, no one on this planet can consistently purchase a stock at its bottom and sell at its top. It might happen in a few instances that after your purchase, the stock starts an upward journey and that you bought the stock when it had bottomed, but that is just a random occurrence and you can't repeat it every time.

Case Study #1: Lancer Container

Lancer Container jumped by around ten times in the year 2021, mainly due to the strong business tailwind of the global container shortage. This shortage continued into 2022 too. However, by June 2022, the stock price declined to Rs 200 from its high of Rs 250 in February 2022. Those who are invested in the stock need to decide whether to continue to hold it, invest more upon price decline or start profit booking.

To decide whether to exit, hold or buy more, let's have a look at the data points we have about the stock.

First, consider the operating (EBITDA) margin trajectory. At the time of writing this book, I have the financial numbers of the company up to the quarter ended March 2022. From Fig. 5.2, it is obvious that the company's profit margin deteriorated in the March 2022 quarter for the first time in the past year. As we have mentioned repeatedly, margin expansion is the most important trigger for a stock turning multibagger, so we need to pay serious attention to margin contraction.

I looked at the promoter shareholding pattern, and it throws up some interesting insights. As per Fig. 5.3, we can see that the promoter group started selling their stake in the October–December 2021 period and continued to do

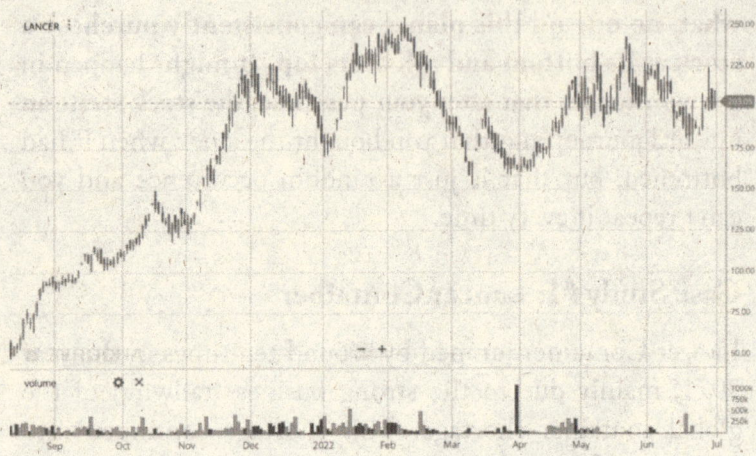

Fig. 5.1: Lancer Container, Stock Price Movement.

(Stock price and EPS in the following section are as per July 2022 data; if the stock undergoes a split or there is a bonus issue after this date, then this data will have to be adjusted accordingly.)

Operating Profit Margin Qtr % of Lancer Container Lines Ltd.

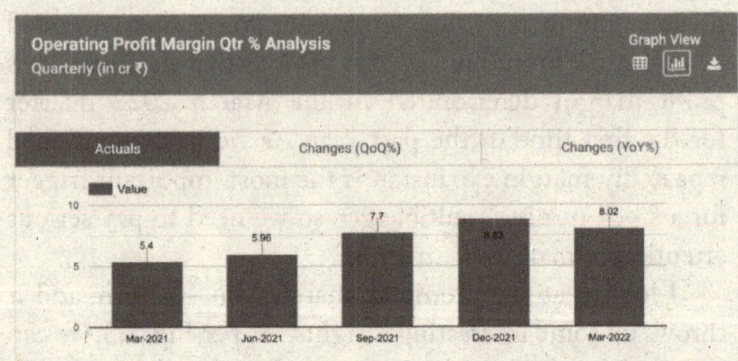

Fig. 5.2: Lancer Container, Operating Margin Trend

so until June 2022. Within the promoter group, the founder and chairman, Abdulkhalik Chataiwala, sold his shares via an open market transaction.

Shareholding Pattern
Numbers in percentages

	Sep 2019	Dec 2019	Mar 2020	Jun 2020	Sep 2020	Dec 2020	Mar 2021	Jun 2021	Sep 2021	Dec 2021	Mar 2022	Jun 2022
Promoters	74.44	74.44	74.44	74.44	74.44	74.44	74.44	74.44	74.44	71.14	70.72	64.01
Abdulkhalik Chataiwala >	39.06	39.06	39.06	51.34	57.82	57.82	57.82	57.82	57.82	57.49	57.49	51.40
Tarannum Chataiwala. >	10.37	10.37	10.37	10.37	10.37	10.37	10.37	10.37	10.37	7.97	7.55	6.92
Badoor Textiles Llc >	4.65	4.65	4.65	4.65	4.65	4.65	4.65	4.65	4.65	4.65	4.65	4.65
Ashwamedh Enterprises Private Limited >	12.28	12.28	12.28	0.00	0.00	0.00	0.00	0.00	0.00	0.00	0.00	0.00
Deepak L Rajani >	6.48	6.48	6.48	6.48	0.00	0.00	0.00	0.00	0.00	0.00	0.00	0.00
Fauzan Abdul Khalik Chataiwala >	1.59	1.59	1.59	1.59	1.59	1.59	1.59	1.59	1.59	1.03	1.03	1.03
Narayanan Kutty Parekattil . >	0.00	0.00	0.00	0.00	0.00	0.00	0.00	0.00	0.00	0.00	0.00	0.00
Deepak Gangadhar Sonar >	0.00	0.00	0.00	0.00	0.00	0.00	0.00	0.00	0.00	0.00	0.00	0.00

Fig. 5.3: Lancer Container, Shareholding Pattern, 2019–22

So, there are now two primary negative data points; margin contraction and stake sale by promoters. On the other hand, the management shared a very optimistic business outlook. Here are excerpts from the management commentary of 23 May 2022:

> . . . Our expectation on freight rate is in line with the outlook of global industry leaders like Maersk, which expect strong rise in freight rates to continue in 2022 amid ongoing pressure on supply chain thereby leading to congestions at port . . . The management expects the revenue to grow by 30% - 40% for FY23, mainly on the account of increase in geographic footprint, sustained high freight rates, new TEUs addition, addition of new customers and aggressive sales strategy . . . EBITDA margin will improve further by 50 to 60 bps due to large operational efficiency and volume

commitment with vessel operators to negotiate on slot charges which is the major component of operational cost.

Overall, we have two different sets of contradicting data points, as follows:

1. Negative points: Margin contraction in March 2022 quarter, stake sale by promoters, and PE ratio having already expanded by more than four times.
2. Positive points: Management expects 30–40 per cent revenue growth in FY2023 with a 50–60 basis points (bps) margin expansion.

When there are contradicting data points, future stock price prediction becomes a difficult task. It is perhaps the most difficult task in investing, and no one can consistently predict the future with 100 per cent success over a long period. My rationale suggests that one should either consider profit booking or continue to hold the stock. My reasons are as follows:

1. Even if the company reports 30–40 per cent revenue growth in FY2023, that would be still lower than the 99 per cent growth that it reported in FY2022. So, the growth rate will slow down. Moving ahead, the strong rise in freight rates can't continue forever; sooner or later they will reverse, and at that point, the growth rate can experience a further slowdown.
2. It can happen that the 30–40 per cent expected growth in FY2023 is already factored in the stock price because the PE ratio has already experienced significant expansion.

Moving forward, the chances of further PE expansion can be tough.

Overall, as per my rationale, the stock price of Lancer Container cannot repeat the performance of 2021 (ten times the return) in the 2022–23 period. Remember, I am writing this in June–July 2022. No one knows how the stock will actually behave in the second half of 2022 and 2023. My expectation can prove wrong. The purpose of this book is not to establish my accuracy in predicting the future but to communicate to you the logical steps of decision-making.

Case Study #2: Chemcrux Enterprises (March 2019–March 2021)

Let's have a look at Fig. 5.4. From March 2019 to March 2021, the stock price jumped by around 100 per cent, but the PE ratio didn't expand at all. In fact, the PE ratio contracted from the 14–15 range to the 10–11 level in the same period. It essentially means that only earnings expansion contributed to the stock price movement.

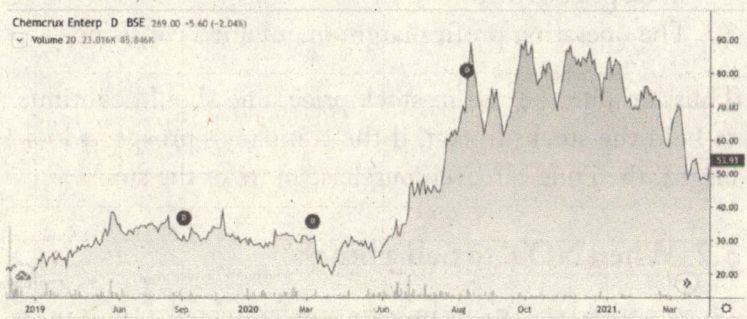

Fig. 5.4: Chemcrux, Stock Price Movement, 2019–21

Now, if we follow the company's EBITDA margin trend from Fig. 5.5, we will find that the margin remained pretty consistent over the FY2019–FY2021 period.

Financial Year	FY 2018	FY 2019	FY 2020	FY 2021
Total Revenue	100.00%	100.00%	100.00%	100.00%
EBITDA ‡	15.84%	24.89%	26.84%	24.74%
PBIT ‡	13.73%	22.63%	24.82%	22.52%
PBT ‡	12.75%	22.13%	24.27%	22.24%
Net Income ‡	7.46%	16.70%	18.21%	16.50%
EPS	1.60	6.29	7.18	6.04

Fig. 5.5: Chemcrux, EBITDA Margin Trend, 2019–21

Summarizing the above data points as of March 2021, we get the following insights:

1. The stock price jumped by around 100 per cent.
2. Despite this jump in stock price, the PE ratio moderated. So, it was earnings expansion that fuelled stock price growth.
3. The operating profit margin maintained consistency.

Thus, despite the rise in stock price, one should continue to hold the stock. In fact, if the company's prospects look bright, then one can even purchase more of the stock.

5.2 When NOT to Sell a Stock

I have noticed that many investors prefer to book profits once a stock generates a certain percentage of returns. That can be a costly mistake. If I had completely sold my shares of Chemcrux Enterprises after obtaining 100 per cent returns, then I would have missed out on 1800 per cent-plus gains afterwards. The same is true for Can Fin Homes, Caplin Point Lab, Lancer Container, and my other multibagger stocks. So, price movement should not be a deciding parameter for selling a stock. You need to forget about the current price and unrealized profit/loss while considering an exit.

> 'Never ever sell a stock just because the price jumped by a certain percentage. Remember, price is just a number; it should not be a deciding factor for selling a stock.'

Often, investors ask when they can sell a stock. I believe more than when to sell it, when not to sell is what we should have a clear idea about. If you know someone who is in the stock market for the last few decades, you will find that at some point he had multibagger stocks like HDFC Bank, Wipro or Page Industries, but he did not hold on to those shares long enough for 50 times or 100 times profit. So, more than stock selection, a proper holding period determines multibagger returns, and for that, you must have a clear idea of when not to sell a stock. Let's explore various conditions that are crucial for making a sell decision.

Better prospects

No matter how much the stock price has appreciated in the past, if the company has a better future outlook, then one should continue to hold the stock. My first investment in Chemcrux was back in March 2017.

By 2021, the stock was showing more than ten times the returns in my portfolio. While I posted a few YouTube videos and wrote Twitter posts about Chemcrux, many investors suggested that I book profits as the stock price had already appreciated a lot. I was determined not to sell my holdings completely, only because of the planned capacity expansion that the company had been working on since 2020. Finally, in June 2022, the company released the following press note:

> . . . The expansion plan is in line with the strategy to enhance the capacities in chemistries handled and expertise. This capacity addition will cater to growing demand from existing customers and developing markets. The expansion plan is expected to be completed over a period of 15 months and would require an approximate investment up to Rs.80 Cr . . . On completion of the expansion as envisaged, the capacity is likely to be doubled.

As per the press release, the installed capacity is likely to double by September 2023. To be on the safe side, if I consider another six to twelve months for optimum utilization of the added capacity, then the overall revenue can be expected to double during calendar year 2024. So, there is still 100 per cent revenue growth visibility over the 2022–24 period. This is why, as of 2022, although the stock has gained by around forty times from my initial investment, I still prefer to hold on to it.

'Irrespective of the jump in stock price, if a company has better prospects, one shouldn't be in hurry to book profits.'

(**Important note:** This is not investment advice or a research report on Chemcrux Enterprises. The same goes for any other stock mentioned in the book. This book is written for educational purposes and is not an investment advisory. Before investing in any stock mentioned in the book, one should conduct one's own due diligence and risk profiling, take responsibility for the profit/loss that will result and consult with a financial adviser. By the time you finish reading this book, I may or may not even be holding the stock. It is not feasible for me to intimate my readers prior to my selling any of my portfolio stocks.)

Earnings expansion in a bear market

If you notice that a particular stock is experiencing consistent earnings expansion despite the overall weakness in the market, then that stock requires extra attention. The 2018–19 period experienced a major bear phase in the small-cap index. Now, suppose, back in 2017, Mohit had invested in five different stocks and at the end of 2019, their performance was as follows:

1. Stock 1: 10 per cent gain
2. Stock 2: 5 per cent gain
3. Stock 3: 30 per cent decline
4. Stock 4: 50 per cent decline
5. Stock 5: 60 per cent decline

At this stage, due to some emergency, Mohit requires to sell some of his holdings. Now, out of these five stocks, which one should be on the priority list for selling? Most investors would think it would be prudent to sell the first and second stocks, as those would fetch Mohit nominal profits. But this would be a very costly mistake. During a bear phase (when the market is declining), a stock price can show some strength only because of earnings expansion. Due to the overall market weakness, the PE ratio experiences either contraction or consolidation. It essentially means that in the future, whenever a bull phase resumes, the PE ratio will expand, helping the stock price to offer multifold returns. Thus, a stock that witnesses moderate gain in a bear phase due to earnings expansion can be a potential multibagger in a bull market when both earnings and PE expansion will kick in. From our example, the first and second stocks are actually potential multibaggers because, despite overall market weakness, their price has been showing some strength. Selling such stocks in a bear phase means throwing away your golden eggs.

'Never sell a stock that is showing earnings expansion despite overall weakness in the market.'

Promoters increasing stake

Promoters are the best persons to predict the future of a business; it is they who know the company inside out. Thus, when promoters increase their stake in their own business, then it calls for extra attention. Broadly speaking, promoters can increase their stake in their companies using two ways:

1. **Open market purchase**: This is normal market purchase, just like your or my investment in any company. The promoter or promoter group can increase their stake in their company by simply purchasing shares from the open market. In this process, the total number of equity shares of the company remains the same but the percentage of promoter shareholding increases. This is considered very positive for any company, whether it is large-cap, mid-cap, small-cap or micro-cap.

2. **Preferential allotment**: In simple language, preferential allotment is when promoters issue new shares to allot to themselves at a price that can be higher or lower than the market price. In this process, additional capital is getting infused into the business, but at the same time, the total number of outstanding shares is also being increased. When the total number of shares of a company increases, it essentially reduces EPS and creates obstacles to PE expansion. Thus, this process is not very beneficial for minority shareholders like you and me.

Overall, in both processes, the percentage shareholding of the promoter increases, but in the preferential allotment process, the total outstanding shares also increase, hurting minority shareholders. Now I might be asked, how can a small investor know whether the increase in promoter shareholding is due to open market purchase or from a preferential issue of shares? Well, in both cases, the promoter needs to disclose these details to the stock exchange. You need to monitor the company-specific 'Corporate Announcement' section on the stock exchange websites. Fig. 5.6 is a grab from the BSE website with this section indicated:

Fig. 5.6: Corporate announcement section of the BSE

When promoters increase their stake in a company via open market purchase, it may not reflect as a big hike in the overall shareholding pattern, but that tiny increase is enough to spark a rally in the stock price. Actually, open market purchase by the promoter triggers great attention towards the stock in question from market participants. It helps in better price discovery. Back in 2013–14, I had invested in a micro-cap stock, Fluidomat, primarily because of an open market purchase done by the promoters. The company manufactures fluid coupling, which has a wide application in the infrastructure sector. Being a small-sized company, there was not enough information on it in the public domain. There were no management interviews/ guidance, no conference calls and no public appearances by the officials. Further, not a single brokerage or research house had active coverage on Fluidomat. Institutional shareholding in the company was nil. Investing in such an unknown micro-cap always carries a certain amount of risk. The stock grabbed my attention because of the increase in promoter holding, along with the fact that it had zero debt and strong ROE and ROCE. The purchase paid off; within one year of my investment, the stock generated returns of over 300 per cent!

Obviously, an increase in promoter stake cannot be the only consideration while investing in a stock. It must be combined with all other parameters. If you notice incremental open market purchases by promoters in one of your existing portfolio stocks, then that can be a great candidate for repeat buying.

'Promoters increasing their stake via open market purchase can be a huge confidence booster for a stock that is showing all other signs of becoming a potential multibagger. One can consider repeat buying of the stock in such instances.'

5.3 When to Sell a Multibagger Stock

Now let's consider some important factors that should trigger a sell decision.

Excessive PE expansion

This is the most important trigger for selling a multibagger stock. PE expansion is one of the primary factors behind multibagger returns. However, PE can't expand indefinitely. When the PE ratio reaches some exorbitant territory, it will begin its journey of contraction or consolidation. Either way, the stock price takes a pause. One shouldn't worry about this, as long as earnings growth is showing encouraging trends. However, the moment earnings growth slows down too, the stock price accelerates on its downward journey. During the PE expansion journey, one needs to monitor similar stocks from the same sector. For example, if the majority of small-cap pharma companies have their PE ratios in the 10–30 zone and one particular stock is in the 40–50 zone, then one should consider profit

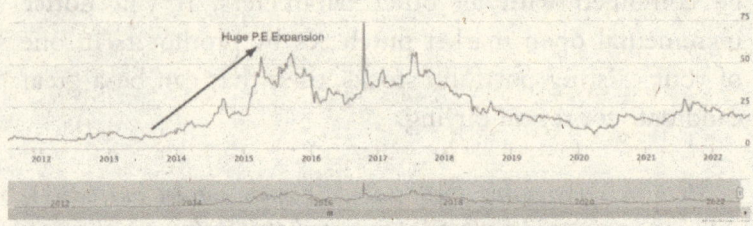

Fig. 5.7: Caplin Point Lab, PE chart, 2012–22

booking on it. Let's have a look at the PE ratio chart of Caplin Point Lab:

As is evident from Fig. 5.7, when I invested in Caplin Point Lab, the PE ratio was hovering at the 10–12 level. Afterwards, by the end of 2016, PE expanded to linger in the 45–50 zone; this meant PE expansion of around five times. During that time, the majority of small-cap pharma companies were available in the 10–30 PE range, so I started profit booking assuming that the PE ratio may not expand beyond the 50–55 level. After my profit booking in 2016, the stock price continued its bull run during all of 2017, but eventually declined a lot over the 2018–20 period while the PE ratio settled in the 15–25 range.

Similarly, when I invested in Can Fin Homes back in 2013, the PE ratio was around 4–5. It jumped to its peak of 35–36 in July 2017 and then started to cool down. I wasn't able to book my profits on the stock at peak PE, but I was under the impression that for a small-cap housing finance company, a 30+ PE ratio was not sustainable at all. I had started booking profits in 2017 and sold my position completely in 2018.

In a similar fashion, while the PE of Lancer Container expanded by more than four times and crossed the 40 levels, I started booking profits because no other similar-sized business was trading at PEs of higher than 30. It is true that after my profit booking, the stock price continued its upward journey, but soon it started to consolidate and the PE ratio cooled down.

The situation was a little different in the case of Chemcrux Enterprises. Although its PE ratio expanded from the 6–8 range in 2017 to the 25–30 zone in 2022, many small-sized speciality chemicals businesses were trading in the same zone. Moreover, in 2022 too, I didn't find any sign of a slowdown in earnings growth; on the contrary, due to the scheduled capacity expansion, earnings could expand even faster in the following years! But should the PE ratio shoot beyond 50, then I might think differently.

Overall, during PE expansion, one needs to monitor the PE ratio of similar stocks and the future earnings growth potential. As long as there is clear visibility of stronger earnings growth, high PEs can sustain, but if there is a slight probability of a growth slowdown, the PE ratio can come under pressure.

'An excessive PE expansion in a stock, beyond those of its peers, and doubt as to future earnings growth are the two primary triggers for selling a multibagger stock.'

Apart from the primary triggers for selling a multibagger stock, there are some auxiliary triggers, which are as follows:

1. **Other, better returns opportunities**: You can sell a stock if you find some better returns opportunities. If there is better returns visibility from other asset classes like real estate, then you can shift from equities to real estate too.

2. **Realization that the investment was a mistake**: If you invest in a company without adequate research or by relying on some external tips or sources and later realize it was a mistake, then you should exit.

3. **Requirement for funds**: One can always book partial profits for fund requirements. In calendar year 2019, I had booked partial profits from Chemcrux to fund my house purchase and marriage expenses. There were no issues with the stock, so I did only partial profit booking. Despite this profit booking, Chemcrux remained the largest holding in my portfolio at that time.

While investing in any stock, always note down your investment reasons. While hunting for multibaggers, write down the potential triggers for earnings and PE expansion. When those triggers are no longer valid, then consider exiting the stock. If your investment reasons are clear to you, then you will never find it difficult to decide your exit.

'If you can write down the precise triggers of buying a stock, then making your exit decision won't be a problem.'

Chapter 6

Idea Generation and Investment Flow

6.1 Introduction

There are around 5000 listed companies in the stock market. One of the most frequently asked questions is: 'Where can I begin my multibagger hunt?' Is any screener available that can shortlist thirty or forty stocks on which one can start further research? Let's understand the basics first. For multibagger returns, you need to shortlist stocks that can have both earnings and PE expansion potential. However, a screener would filter out stocks based on past parameters. A screener can easily give you a list of stocks with profit margins of more than, say, 15 per cent or 20 per cent. It can also tell you which stocks experienced margin expansion in the last few years. But can a screener notify you of a list of stocks with future margin expansion potential? Just because a stock experienced margin expansion in the last few quarters doesn't necessarily mean that the same trend will continue in the future; rather, a few quarters of margin expansion are often followed by margin contraction. In my bestselling book *How to Avoid Loss and Earn Consistently in the Stock Market*, I have shared detailed screening parameters that have proved quite beneficial in selecting potential 'outperformers' from among the high-volume mid-cap and large-cap stocks. But when it comes to small-cap and micro-cap stocks from the SME segment, the lack of sufficient data on them becomes a big hurdle. The reasons are as follows:

1. Unlike mainboard stocks that publish their financial results every three months, SME companies are required to publish only half-yearly financial results.

2. Due to this six-month gap in getting to know their financials, any company data captured by the screeners quickly becomes outdated. For example, if you run a screener through the micro-cap SME segment in the month of August–September, it will fetch data based on March-ending financial numbers.

3. Due to the outdated data, by the time a screener captures a stock, it becomes too late for investing in it—i.e., the stock might have already generated multifold returns by then.

4. Due to these same reasons, none of my notable multibaggers like Chemcrux, Lancer, Sirca Paints, Prevest DenPro, Gujarat Themis, etc., were discovered using a screener.

'*A screener is an excellent tool for researching high-volume stocks; however, for low-volume SME stocks that publish only half-yearly financial numbers, the lack of sufficient data is a big hurdle when it comes to choosing a stock for investment.*'

Now let's explore how I generate investment ideas and use decision flow in multibagger hunting. I have also included two of my recent stock picks to illustrate decision flow in multibagger hunting.

6.2 Idea Generation

The most straightforward way to hunt for multibaggers is to scan all the upcoming IPOs in the BSE SME and NSE SME segments. Every year, around 40–70 SME companies get listed. Now, how can one scan all these companies, one may ask? But I have been doing exactly this since 2017 and quite comfortably. In fact, all my notable multibagger stocks, such as Chemcrux Enterprises, Lancer Container, Sirca Paints and Bajaj Healthcare, were discovered while scanning SME IPOs. Remember, more than 90 per cent of SME IPOs are just trash. The trick lies in how quickly one can reject a stock to move on to the next name. Here is an example to illustrate how this can be done:

In October 2021, while I was scanning all the upcoming IPOs on the SME platform, a small company, Destiny Logistics and Infrastructure, grabbed my attention. Here is the summarized write-up about the business:

Incorporated in 2011, Destiny Logistics and Infra Limited provide logistics services i.e. land-based transportation via 3rd party service providers. It offers a wide range of services i.e. packaging, loading, transportation, unloading, and unpacking of items to offer end-to-end solutions. The company's operations are concentrated in the domestic market, more particularly, in the state of West Bengal.

The business has further diversified into the infrastructure development activity and started the 'Construction of Storm Water Drainage Scheme Project' in West Bengal. The total contract value awarded is Rs. 58.27 crores.

Competitive strengths

- A comprehensive range of transportation services and diversification in infrastructure development.
- Well-defined organizational structure.
- Managerial expertise and smooth operational flow.

Anything attractive that grabbed your attention yet? I guess your answer is 'no'. Now, here come the company financials:

On the financial performance front, for the last three fiscals, the company has posted a total revenue/net profit of Rs. 6.73 cr. / Rs. 0.05 cr. (FY19), Rs. 6.75 cr. / Rs. 0.05 cr. (FY20) and Rs. 10.06 cr. / Rs. 0.30 cr. (FY21).

Once you combine the reported financials and order book, then the data becomes interesting. The company posted a total revenue of Rs 10 crore in FY2021, and the current order-book size is Rs 58.27 crore! That means there is clear visibility of a six-time revenue jump! This data was sufficient for me to get excited about the company as a potential multibagger. Should I invest in it outright? Or should I dig deeper for a complete analysis?

Well, within the next five to ten minutes I discovered that, forget about investing in it, this company was not even worth spending a few hours of my time on for detailed research! Here are the reasons:

- For execution of the Rs 58-crore order book, the company would either opt for external borrowings or would dilute equity capital or resort to both.
- If the company opts for external borrowings (bank loan), then the interest expense would affect the profit margin, which means earnings can't jump by six times in sync with revenue growth.
- If the company opts for equity dilution (like rights issues, FPO, etc.) then the total number of shares will increase, which means EPS will reduce.
- If the company opts to do both, then it will be a double blow to earnings.
- Now, recall what we learnt in chapter 2: 'Despite revenue growth, without earnings expansion, a stock can't generate multifold returns.'
- In this case, despite clear visibility of six times revenue growth, there is no visibility of similar earnings expansion, so I rejected the stock outright.

Apart from all this, the balance sheet and cash flow statement of the company were not encouraging. Execution risk would always be at play because the company was going to execute a project that was valued at six times its current revenue. Would it be able to complete the project within the given time, given its resources? That was doubtful.

Overall, within just five to ten minutes of exploring the company further, I had a long list of facts about it that could have gone against the multibagger journey, and I rejected the stock to move ahead to researching the next name. The quicker you can do this exercise, the easier it will be to cover the maximum number of stocks. Obviously, during my initial years, I was not very quick in decision-making, but over a period of time, I have improved. So, don't get disheartened if it took a few hours for you to decide which stock to invest in. Only experience can make you faster at this exercise.

Quick checklist for rejection of a stock

Question	Answer
Are you finding it difficult to understand the business?	Yes/No
Is it difficult for the business to scale (grow)?	Yes/No
Does the business require huge borrowings to fuel growth?	Yes/No
Does the business have no pricing power or competitive advantage?	Yes/No
Is it a cyclical business?	Yes/No
Is there any corporate fraud associated with the company?	Yes/No
Did the company inflate its financials just before its IPO?	Yes/No

If any of the answers to these questions is 'yes', then it is better to avoid the stock and move on to the next name.

6.3 Investment Flow of My Multibaggers

To elaborate on my idea generation and the investment flow process I follow, I have decided to write about two of my recent investments, made at the time of publication of this book, hoping for multibagger returns. It would be a huge mistake for you to consider it as a stock recommendation and to invest blindly in these two stocks. Even if these two stocks generate multifold returns for me, there is no guarantee that you, too, can make money from them. Rather, there is a high probability of your losing money. Once you complete this book, you will understand why blind investment using borrowed ideas mostly leads to losses.

> *The objective of this book is not to spoon-feed you but rather to teach you the process so that you can feed yourself for the rest of your life.*

No author will dare to write about the future multibagger potential of stocks because they fear that if these stocks fail to deliver, then their readers will start mocking them publicly. No one would like to lose their reputation. Readers need to understand that participating in the stock market is not like solving a mathematical problem; rather, it's all about predicting the future on the basis of current facts and figures. Any prediction always comes with uncertainty, and this is why even the most successful investor on the planet can't consistently make correct future predictions. It will be your fault if you expect someone to predict the future with 100 per cent accuracy on a consistent basis. The same set of information is available to everyone. It is not that veteran investors can access a particular bit of information that you can't. The Internet has removed information barriers. Back in the 1990s, retail investors were deprived of basic information for equity research, but today the situation is completely different. Whatever data a mutual fund manager of FIIs can access, the same can be accessed by a new investor too. What sets apart a successful investor from the rest is his or her rational decision-making ability while keeping emotions aside. Thus, it is not important whether a prediction comes true or not. Wealth creation depends on the quality of the decision-making process. The following case studies will help you understand the decision flow process.

Case Study #1: Prevest DenPro

Prevest DenPro first came to my notice at the time of its IPO in September 2021. The idea of examining this stock came from my continuous tracking of every IPO on the BSE SME and NSE SME platforms. SME IPO tracking is a very boring and time-consuming process, because only two or three IPOs out of 100 are worthy of investing in. To give you perspective, in the calendar year 2021, a total of sixty-five companies issued IPOs on the SME platform. I scanned all of them and found only two worthy of detailed research. Out of these two, I am comfortable holding only one company over the longer term, and that is Prevest DenPro.

Incorporated in 2000 by Atul Modi, Prevest DenPro, headquartered in Jammu, is into the development and manufacture of dental products used for the diagnosis, prevention and treatment of dental conditions. The company develops, manufactures and markets a comprehensive portfolio of dental materials for diagnosing, treating and preventing dental conditions. The company has a portfolio of more than 100 products and sells them via distributors in the export as well as domestic markets.

Once I went through the profile of the company, the questions that came to my mind were as follows:

- What's special about the company?
- Is it doing something different, something unique, that no one else is doing?
- There are no other similar companies listed on the Indian stock market. Why is that?
- Does the company have a moat or competitive advantage?

After a detailed Google search and a reading of the draft red herring prospectus (DRHP), I came to the conclusion that the industry is fragmented. Global players in similar business lines include Danaher Corporation, Dentsply Sirona, Voco, Institut Straumann AG, Osstem Implant Co. Ltd, Zimmer Biomet, Medicept UK, Mani Inc., Kavo GC, Ivoclar Vivadent, Nobel Biocare, 3M, GC Dental, Shofu Dental, etc. There are many domestic players too in similar businesses (such as Prime Dental Products, Orikam Healthcare, Dental Avenue, Vishal Dentocare and D-Tech Orthodontics). However, none of them is large enough to dominate the market. This is why there is not a single listed player in the Indian stock market. Global giants like 3M are selling a similar range of products but at a higher cost. Many dentists still prefer dental products from the global brands, which are priced higher than those of domestic brands like Prevest. So, there is nothing unique, nothing special, about the company. However, a quick look at the financials of the company revealed the following:

1. Both revenue and profit were growing at a very fast pace while the company had negligible debt in its books.
2. Operating profit margin improved every year since FY2018, and at the time of the IPO, it was 28 per cent (FY2021 figure), which is considered very healthy.
3. Excellent ROE and ROCE. The last four-year average ROE stood at over 30 per cent, and average ROCE at over 40 per cent.
4. Healthy cash flows from operation, low debt-to-equity ratio, high interest coverage ratio and fair tax rate. There was nothing to complain about.
5. Interestingly, the IPO was priced at Rs 84, which was approximately thirteen times of FY2021 earnings. A PE ratio of 13 is very attractive for a company with such a financial track record.

(Stock price and EPS in this section are as per June 2022 data; if the stock undergoes split or bonus after June 2022, then this data will have to be adjusted accordingly).

Looking at the attractiveness of the offer price, I applied for the IPO. At the end of the last bidding day, the IPO was oversubscribed by 38 times overall. The retail portion was oversubscribed by 32 times; the non-institutional investors (NII) portion by 78.98 times and the qualified institutional buyer (QIB) portion by 5.78 times. The oversubscription figure indicated the following:

1. I would not receive the desired allotment.
2. There was indeed something positive about the company.

I got an allotment of 1600 shares at Rs 84 each, which is obviously much less than the quantity I had applied for. On the day of listing, the stock price jumped to Rs 190. Thus, an instant 100 per cent appreciation. I didn't book profits, but rather dug deeper into the business over the next month. The focus is now to figure out the possibility of earnings and PE expansion. After the listing, as the stock price doubled instantly, the PE ratio also doubled, reaching the 26–28 zone. The critical point to gauge is the probability of further PE expansion. After detailed research from various sources over the next month, my observations were as follows:

- The company had an existing manufacturing facility of over 27,000 sq. ft in area with a capacity of 200 metric tonnes per annum (MTPA). With the IPO fund of Rs 18 crore, it was setting up another 16,000 sq. ft plant for hygiene products (sanitizers and disinfectants), oral hygiene products (mouthwashes and mouth rinses), oral care products (medicated ointments, gels and creams for dental treatment) and bio-materials (bone grafting materials and membranes). The expansion would be sufficient to fuel revenue growth over the next three to four years.

- As the expansion would be mainly funded by the IPO money, it would not increase the debt in its books. There would be no increased interest burden that could pose a challenge during uncertain times.

- The company had a track record of more than twenty years. Historically, it had managed growth very well while maintaining minimal debt in its books.

- The company has United States Food and Drug Administration (USFDA) approval for five products but was yet to start business in the US and Canada. It was waiting for more approvals from USFDA so that it could enter the US market with a sizeable number of products. The profit margins in the US and Canadian markets were much higher than those from the Indian market. So, whenever the company started selling in the US, that would open up an excellent profit margin expansion opportunity.

- Moreover, the company was focusing on penetrating more export markets, such as Saudi Arabia, the UAE and other countries in the Middle East, Brazil and Australia. Profit margins from the export business are much higher than from the domestic market.

- When a company successfully implements the strategy of 'Make in India and Sell Globally', it creates enormous wealth for shareholders. Back in 2014–16, Caplin Point Lab had generated multifold returns on my investment with this same strategy. Here, Prevest had a manufacturing facility in Jammu where there was no shortage of cheap labour or natural resources. Manufacturing in Jammu and selling worldwide seemed an excellent value proposition for me. (Jammu is quite peaceful compared with the Kashmir region. Manufacturing facilities there have never faced any threat in the last twenty years, while adjoining Kashmir witnesses frequent terror attacks and political instability.)

- For the financial year ended March 2021, the total revenue amounted to Rs 27 crore, and the management's target was to double revenue in another three to four years. The total revenue figure of Rs 27 crore was not a big sum. Even without any kind of management guidance, an investor could see that the low base effect could drive exponential revenue growth.

- The main raw materials required to manufacture dental products include zinc oxide, pumice powder, aluminium chloride, camphor, glycerine, paraffin, zirconium oxide, eugenol, diatomaceous earth and waxes, all of which were mainly sourced from domestic suppliers.

- Despite the volatility in its raw material prices, the company's historical margin trend suggested that it could successfully pass on any kind of raw material price hikes to the end customers. The customer is the dentist community who can further successfully pass on any price hike to their end customers (patients). We all know that dental patients have no bargaining power. Suppose you went to a reputed dental clinic for root canal treatment and the clinic tells you what it will cost. Do you bargain over the price? If affordability is in question, then one opts for a different clinic, but I have never seen a patient bargaining over charges at a clinic or hospital.

- Thus, despite being in a fragmented industry that had many players, almost all the companies in this business held some sort of pricing power.

- The founder of the company, Atul Modi, aged sixty-seven, and his wife, Namrata Modi, aged sixty-three, might remain at the helm of the company for another ten to fifteen years. However, their daughter, Niharika Modi, aged thirty-seven, was already a board member. So the second generation was already being groomed to handle the business. Moreover, the company had appointed professionals to take care of overseas expansion, research and development, etc. So the business was not completely dependent on the founding family, which was a good sign.

From the above observations, my conclusions were as follows:

1. There was a huge addressable market size for the company to capitalize on for earnings expansion.
2. Geographical expansion into export markets, capacity addition and regulatory approvals, all were in place for earnings growth.
3. Despite the capacity expansion, the company maintained a negligible debt position and healthy cash flows from its operations.

4. Its ability to pass on any input price hikes, its asset-light business model and its entry into the high-margin export business meant that there was still a high possibility of margin expansion that would boost earnings.

5. The stock being in the SME segment, traded in lot size, had still not been properly discovered among the majority of market participants, so the chances of PE expansion remained.

The next question that came to my mind was how much the PE ratio could expand. What would be a fair range of PE multiple for the company? After the stock market listing, the company started commanding a PE ratio of 26–28. So from here on, what could be the potential upside? There was no similar business listed on the stock market, so a direct comparison was not possible. I was looking for a broad match and noticed the company Poly Medicure, which is in the business of manufacturing medical devices. It had commanded an average PE ratio of nearly 40–50 in the last five years. Poly Medicure had a market capitalization of around Rs 7000 crore while Prevest was at Rs 350 crore, so the comparison was not apple-to-apple. However, just taking it as some sort of reference, I concluded that in the case of Prevest, PE expansion was still possible from the 26–28 level. Moreover, after analysing all data points, it looked like a 20–30 per cent CAGR in earnings over the next three to four years might not be an uphill task. And if similar EPS expansion became a reality, then I would not worry about the PE ratio.

'The sustainability of a higher PE ratio and further valuation expansion depend on profit margin and EPS expansion.'

The stock ticked almost every parameter essential for multibagger returns. Thus, I increased my investment in it in November 2021 while the stock price was around Rs 220. Although this price was significantly higher than the IPO price of Rs 84, I still didn't hesitate to invest a significant amount at this level.

Shortly after that, the company posted superior financial numbers for the quarter ended December 2021. The stock price jumped from the Rs 220 level in November 2021 to Rs 450 in January 2022. I didn't book profits on it because the business prospects of the company looked bright. Afterwards, in sync with the broader market decline, the stock price gradually dropped from Rs 450 to Rs 272 by the end of June 2022. In the meanwhile, the company released another set of strong numbers for the financial year ended March 2022. Total revenue jumped by around 37 per cent while net profit witnessed a whopping 55 per cent growth backed by margin expansion. Healthy cash flows from operations continued, with a net debt-free balance sheet. ROE moderated due to the jump in equity capital from the IPO funds but was still maintained at over 20 per cent. The management commentary was equally strong. Thus, overall, despite a sharp drop in the stock price, the company's business prospects were improving further. So, I increased my investment further, to around Rs 300–350, during the April–June 2022 period. At the time of writing this book, here are the three probable outcomes I can visualize from this investment:

Probability 1 (Best-case scenario)

The company continues its successful penetration into high-margin export markets. In such a situation, earnings (EPS) expansion will be faster than revenue expansion. Within the next three to four years, the expanded capacity will reach its optimum utilization level, making way for a consistent 25–30 per cent CAGR in earnings. I have noticed that businesses that can grow consistently at more than 25 per cent for four to five years command very high PE ratios, because out of 5000 listed stocks, less than 0.5 per cent display such consistent performance. There are many instances of companies reporting a 40 per cent earnings growth in a particular year and then in the next year reporting that growth has dropped to 5 per cent. This kind of erratic performance typically results in PE ratio contraction. Consistency is the key here.

Overall, a 30 per cent CAGR in EPS for five consecutive years means the EPS would expand by close to four times, and in such a case, PE doubling can become a reality, making way for around ten times the returns from the stock over four to five years. Remember that this is the best possible outcome. While investing, I never set my expectations at the 'best possible' level, but rather, concentrate more on the worst possible outcome.

Probability 2 (Moderate scenario)

The company continues its expansion drive but struggles to successfully penetrate the high-margin markets of the US, Canada, Australia, etc. It is never easy to compete with well-established global brands in the export market. Global brands with deep pockets spend a lot on marketing and promotion. So, unless and until the product range of Prevest proves to be a cheaper but quality alternative, the company will struggle to penetrate the export market. Without an incremental contribution from the export market, the profit margin won't improve, and neither will EPS. The first and foremost criteria for multibagger returns are margin and EPS expansion. Without margin expansion, the PE ratio too can contract. In the absence of margin expansion, revenue growth can prevent the share price from a drastic fall but can't ensure a multibagger stock. In such a scenario, occasional volatility will be noticed and the price might dip by 30–40 per cent or even more from its recent peak. Even without margin expansion, if the company can utilize the new capacity to its optimum level over the next three or four years, then the story might end with moderate returns, maybe yielding 15–20 per cent CAGR in returns on the stock price. Do remember that the occasional sharp downturns in the stock price will instil fear among many investors and some will exit at a loss.

Probability 3 (Worst-case scenario)

Let's look at the worst possible things that can happen to the company.

1. Country-specific regulatory restrictions on products of the company.
2. Regulatory restrictions on the manufacturing facilities of the company.
3. Broader market remains muted over the next few years.

Any kind of regulatory restriction can completely change the growth trajectory of the company. Forget about margin expansion, such a situation will affect revenue growth itself. If news of regulatory restrictions surfaces, then we need to figure out whether the effect will be temporary or permanent and decide to act accordingly.

If the broader market continues to be in a bad phase in addition to these regulatory restrictions, then that would deal a double blow to the stock price. In such a situation, the price will remain under pressure and one can see a drawdown of 40–50 per cent or even more. Exiting from the investment will become very difficult. With proper planning, I might still make an exit at no loss-no profit or at least minimize my losses, but those who invest in the stock blindly will surely end up losing money. Moreover, irrespective of the quantum of my loss, with the knowledge and experience I possess, I can easily recover this loss from my other investments. However, if you lose money after some blind copy-paste work, then you can't recover your losses and will blame me!

(*Important note: The stocks mentioned are not for investment advice or a research report. This book is written for educational purposes and not for offering investment advice. Before investing in any stock mentioned in the book, one should conduct one's own due diligence and risk profiling, take responsibility for any profit/loss that may result and consult with a financial adviser. By the time you read this book, I may or may not continue holding the stocks mentioned in this book. It is not feasible to offer any kind of intimation to all readers prior to selling any of my portfolio stocks. Readers should not expect any statements from me on the prospects of any stock mentioned in the book.*)

Case Study #2: Beta Drugs

Beta Drugs manufactures a wide range of oncology (anti-cancer) drugs and APIs. The stock first came to my notice in 2021. As the stock price was continuing its sharp upward journey at the time, I kept tracking the stock until the price witnessed a sharp dip, in tandem with the broader market, when I finally bought it over June–July 2022. The stock grabbed my attention in the first place for the following reasons:

1. Since FY2018, the company has maintained average annual revenue growth of over 30 per cent.
2. During the same period, the company maintained a healthy EBITDA margin in the range of 18–21 per cent.
3. Earnings growth maintained a healthy track record.
4. ROE and ROCE were both maintained at around 20 per cent.
5. The company opted for multiple expansion projects but maintained overall debt at a very comfortable level. Over the last three years, the debt-to-equity ratio showed a declining trend with an incremental interest coverage ratio, which is a very good sign.

So, there was nothing much to complain about, going by its past financials. Upon further research, I realized the company had some sort of moat because of the strict regulatory compliance required for its product range. It is not easy for any other company to instantly start manufacturing the same set of products. Without a competitive advantage, a small company can't keep reporting such strong growth rates while maintaining a strong balance sheet. Now, the most important point to look at is what the future holds. I kept searching to understand the company's potential for earnings and PE ratio expansion and was able to access an excellent conference call by analysts with the management. Here are the edited excerpts from what the management said:

'We have a clear roadmap to achieve 30 per cent growth annually. The roadmap has also been designed and framed for the next five years . . . Current market size is around Rs 4750 crores and our market share is 3.75 per cent . . . So if we see the product launches, if we had done, that is around nine products last year, then before that three products, this year also we will be doing around eight products. We have a list ready for thirty-five new molecules, which are becoming operated by 2025 . . . we are available in all major leading hospitals in the country, not only the corporate hospitals, but even the government hospitals we are available . . . What we have seen from our calculations [is] that we can do a turnover of Rs 300–350 crore from this current capacity. Taking it forward, as I told you that we have acquired land, there we got the approval, not only to make intermediate, we can have as many blocks as we want, we can have a new formulation plant there, we can have a new API plant there, we can have two separate blocks for intermediates. So expansion plan has also been on a roll and for that the work had already started, the land has already been acquired . . . we are working very hard in penetrating tier-2 and tier-3 cities, which has given rich dividends to us in the past and it will remain in the focus for coming years down the line.

And lastly, we want to focus on haematology segment and gain good market share there.'
(Management commentary as of April 2022)

We can conclude the following from the above commentary:

1. The management has a very aggressive target of 30 per cent annual growth for the next three to four years.
2. Such a growth target raises the next question as to whether there is enough headroom or not in the overall market.
3. The company reported total sales of Rs 184 crore for the financial year ending March 2022, while the total market size is around Rs 4750 crore. This means the overall market size is around twenty-five times bigger than the company's reported sales. So, there is enough headroom for the growth the company has in mind.
4. The current capacity at full utilization is sufficient for 100 per cent revenue growth over the next three to four years. Beyond that, for further capacity addition, the company has already purchased land and has approval for expansion. The capacity addition didn't increase its debt burden, which is a big positive.
5. Growth triggers are new product launches, incremental capacity and penetration into new geographies, which can mostly be funded through internal accruals.

So, revenue growth may not be an issue for the company. Now, the most important point to note is whether revenue growth will accompany margin growth.

If operating profit margin (EBITDA) keeps growing, then earnings will grow faster than revenue and can trigger PE ratio expansion too. The following are edited excerpts from the management commentary that I find beneficial as an answer to the margin expansion question:

'We have just started in all the semi-regulated countries. So, our target is to cater to all the regulated markets after this, that is Europe, then we will be focusing only on the Latin, CIS through all these different accreditations . . . By 2023–24 we will achieve our presence in many of the regulated countries . . . So we see the EBITDA margin to be landing somewhere between 26 per cent to 27 per cent four years down the line. It can be more also since we will be penetrating more of the international market. So, in international markets, you can understand how much revenue and how much the price differences are there as compared to the Indian market. So that market is totally vacant for us. So we will be targeting mainly the export. So, in three, four years down the line EBITDA margins 100 per cent will be on a higher side . . . Then one important factor why we have grown with this percentage is backwardly integrated. We are actually one of the very few companies in India who are backwardly integrated. So, there are a very few companies who are manufacturing API and formulations both . . . Then the cost inflation is definitely there, but on the same side, we are getting a smoother run over the increasing cost for the customer end also. So the only advantage we have right now is that, as I told you, we are backwardly integrated, so we do not have to be so worried about the API costs, because API is one thing which is making it sustainable, which is making it more profitable. So Beta can add up more margins

*after developing new and innovative molecules through its
API company.'*
(Management commentary as of April 2022)

The commentary yields some interesting insights:

1. The company is actively looking for expansion in export
   markets, both semi-regulated and regulated. We know
   that profit margins from the export market are always
   higher than in the domestic market. Increasing revenue
   contribution from the export market always helps in
   margin expansion. I have already seen this happening
   in the case of Caplin Point Lab. Thus, if Beta Drugs
   succeeds in the export market, then a Caplin-like
   multibagger story is a possibility.
2. The management is quite confident about increasing
   the operating (EBITDA) profit margin. Every year it
   is targeting a 1 percentage-point incremental EBITDA
   margin from the previous year.
3. Backward integration and less dependency on raw
   materials from external players can help in margin
   expansion. According to the management, there are
   not many companies that manufacture both APIs and
   formulations. Thus, input price hikes for APIs can
   be passed on to the formulations (end products). The
   company may not pass on 100 per cent of input price
   inflation, but even if it can pass on most of it, then its
   profit margin won't be affected much.

Overall, if I summarize everything, I am getting a niche
and specialized business (anti-cancer drug manufacturer)

that has some sort of a business moat and has big expansion plans ahead. The management is targeting 30 per cent annual revenue growth every year for the next four to five years, with realistic margin expansion possibilities. The field is all set for margin and earnings expansion.

The only issue was that by 2022, the stock price had already moved up more than nine times from its IPO listing price of Rs 103 in 2017. Although I had been tracking the stock since 2021, the sharp upward stock price movement until April 2022 restricted me from investing in it. Then, in June–July 2022, along with the broader market decline, the stock price witnessed a slide of around 30 per cent over just three months. The trailing PE ratio peaked at around 50 and then cooled down to the 23–26 range by July 2022. It is well known that PE expansion is an essential trigger for multibagger returns. I would have never invested in the stock if the PE ratio had remained in the 40–50 range because from that range it is unlikely that it can double. Very few large-caps and mid-caps trade at 80–100 PE, but for small-cap stocks, this is unlikely. However, from the PE range of 23–26, a quality pharma company can further re-rate. Thus, I completed my allocation in June–July itself, unlike in the case of Prevest DenPro, where I invested in parts with improving prospects.

As I write this book, I foresee three probabilities with my investment in Beta Drugs.

Probability 1 (Best-case scenario)

- As per the management guidance, the company continues its 30 per cent revenue growth every year for the next three or four years with margin expansion.

- The company successfully penetrates the high-margin export market.
- Any kind of raw material price volatility is successfully passed on to the end customer.
- The broader market remains supportive, with a rally in the small-cap index.

If all of the above happen, then over the next three to five years, the stock can witness around three to four times EPS expansion along with PE expansion, resulting in a five to six times jump in the stock price.

Probability 2 (Moderate scenario)

- The company maintains its growth journey but the growth rate is lower than the management guidance of 30 per cent.
- Margin expansion is not turning out to be a reality, unlike what the management expected.
- The broader market consolidation continues; there is neither a strong bull run nor a bear phase visible.

In such a scenario, the PE ratio can't expand; rather, it might contract. The stock price might move in tandem with earnings growth.

Probability 3 (Worst-case scenario)

- Regulatory bans or restrictions delay new product launches, hampering growth.
- The profit margin keeps contracting with muted sales figures.

- The company fails to capture the export market.
- The broader market enters a bear phase.

Under these conditions, the investment will turn sour. The stock price will remain under pressure and can witness a drawdown of 30–60 per cent or more. Exiting will become tricky. The target should then be to minimize losses.

Important Note

I would like to remind you again, don't invest blindly in any of the stocks mentioned in the book. Instead of attempting blind copy-paste investment, if you can learn the principles and apply them in the coming days, then I am sure this book that has cost you a few hundred rupees will yield you multifold returns. I am sure about this because, if I had come across similar guidance in my early days of investing, then I might have multiplied my wealth even faster. My attempt is to equip you with knowledge and insights so that after some years, you can master the art of picking multibaggers by yourself. On my website, www. prasenjitpaul.com, I keep sharing insights and rationales on my potential multibagger stocks so that it can empower investors to think independently and over a period of a year, succeed in multibagger hunting by themselves.

'If you give a man a fish, you feed him for a day. If you teach a man to fish, you feed him for a lifetime.'

Chapter 7

Important Points to Remember

7.1 Respect the Market

There is a famous Gujarati phrase, '*Bhav Bhagwan Che*', which means 'price is God'. In other words, the phrase implies that the market is always correct and that the market price is one of the most critical factors to consider while investing in a stock. I realized the importance of that phrase after my investment in Dr Lalchandani Lab turned sour.

Back in May 2018, the SME IPO of Dr Lalchandani Lab grabbed my attention. Established in 1986 by pathologist Arjan Lalchandani, the company offers diagnostic and healthcare-related tests, mainly in Delhi NCR, and has a good reputation and brand value. Arjan Lalchandani is over sixty-five years old. It was his son, Mohit Lalchandani, a man in his thirties, who was instrumental in taking the company public. Diagnostics as a sector always possesses a bright future. The industry as a whole was growing at

16–18 per cent, while the organized segment was expected to grow at 20 per cent. Peers like Dr Lal PathLabs, Thyrocare, Metropolis, etc., were growing in double digits and commanding PE multiples of 40–50. Dr Lalchandani Lab came out with an IPO priced at around eighteen times the PE ratio. Here is the brief investment checklist:

Earnings expansion drivers (as of May 2018)

- **Huge opportunity size**: The total market size of the diagnostics sector was a few thousand crore, while the company had total sales of only Rs 2.8 crore and net profit of less than Rs 1 crore. Dr Lal PathLabs was clocking over Rs 1000 crore in sales and over Rs 170 crore in profit, like many of the larger companies in the segment. Thus, the opportunity size was huge.
- **Geographical expansion**: Dr Lalchandani Lab had a presence only in the Delhi–NCR area. With the IPO money, it could easily set up a few more labs outside Delhi and multiply profitability quickly.
- **Low base effect**: Any company with only Rs 2.8 crore in revenue can easily turn into a Rs 20–30 crore company. In the case of Dr Lalchandani Lab, if they set up ten to twelve laboratories over two or three years, then within five years, the revenue numbers were bound to soar by eight to ten times.

PE expansion drivers (as of May 2018)

- **Valuation gap with peers**: Dr Lalchandani Lab came out with an IPO at a PE of around 18, while peers like Thyrocare, Lal PathLabs and later, Metropolis Healthcare, traded in the 40–60 PE range. Obviously, being a very small player, Dr Lalchandani cannot be expected to trade at a PE of 40–50. However, even if the PE expanded from 18-plus to the 25–26 range, then too the stock would become a multibagger.

• **Margin expansion**: If the company can set up more laboratories and sample collection centres, then economies of scale would kick in, resulting in margin expansion.

• **Little-discovered stock**: Being a BSE-SME listed company, hardly anyone was aware of the company. Further, with its market capitalization of only Rs 15–20 crore, it was impossible for any brokerage house or fund manager to track the stock.

Overall, Dr Lalchandani Lab had every ingredient to become a multibagger stock. However, since the IPO listing, the stock never sustained above the IPO price of Rs 30. Further, throughout 2018 and 2019, the stock price continued its downward journey.

My mistake

I had invested in the IPO at Rs 30 and, at around the same time, had visited their Delhi office in the Greater Kailash area, which is also their primary diagnostics centre. What also inspired me is the fact that back then I had noticed it had mostly five-star reviews on Google and on its Facebook page.

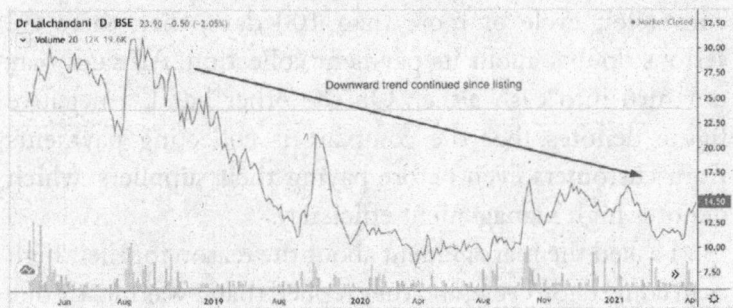

Fig. 7.1: Historical Price Chart of Dr Lalchandani Lab

What was wrong with the business?

Despite the huge opportunity size, untapped market, expansion plans, low base and valuation gap with the competitors, the stock price disappointed. I had hoped for PE expansion. However, the PE ratio contracted from 18-plus to 10–11, and in a few months went below 10.

A close look at their balance sheet suggested the problem lay in their 'cash conversion cycle'. Let's understand this metric first. The cash conversion cycle is the number of days that a company requires to convert its resources into cash through sales. Remember, 'sales' and 'cash' are two different things. It might happen that a business records sales but receives payment for them after a certain number of days. A higher cash conversion cycle means the funds are getting blocked or tied up in the business, which means the business is struggling to collect cash. The cash conversion cycle of Dr Lalchandani Lab stood at more than 100 days, whereas for peers like Dr Lal PathLabs and Metropolis the number was negative. If any business reports a cash conversion cycle of more than 100 days, then there are serious doubts about its payment collection. All sales may not turn into cash either. On the other hand, a negative figure denotes that the company is collecting payments from customers even before paying their suppliers, which denotes high management efficiency.

I asked the management about the reason for their high cash conversion cycle, and they replied that it was mostly due to the Government of India's Central Government Health Scheme (CGHS). The payment cycle was often delayed by many months and a big chunk of the company's revenue depended on this government scheme, which was not going to reverse any time soon. Afterwards, I realized how low the probability of the stock turning into a multibagger was and started selling it in small quantities during every up move. Before 2020, I had sold out 50 per cent of my holding in the stock, and the remaining 50 per cent was sold at some profit due to the COVID tailwind. Every diagnostics business enjoyed massive tailwinds during the peak COVID period as a result of RT-PCR testing. Although the government had capped the price of RT-PCR tests, the huge volume of testing helped all diagnostics businesses. The same applied to Dr Lalchandani Lab too. The company reported its best-ever quarterly performance during the April–September 2021 period when the second wave peaked in India. That one-off incident helped the stock price reach the Rs 40–50 level. I sold off the remaining 50 per cent investment in it at a profit, minimizing my overall loss from the stock. Without the COVID tailwind, my overall loss from buying the stock would have been much higher.

The important point to note here is that the tanking of a stock following its IPO listing is a signal for caution. Even without the analysis and my discovery of the company's cash conversion cycle, if I had strictly followed what the stock price movement was communicating, then I could have avoided repeat buying of the stock.

Since then, I have followed these two simple strategies that have turned out to be very impactful:

1. **Never ever average stocks on their downward journey**
2. **Never buy any stock at its 52-week low.**

> *'Don't invest in a stock if the price hits new 52-week lows continually.'*

7.2 Price Is Just a Number

The stock price in absolute terms carries no significance in the context of multibagger returns. Just because a stock price doubled in the last few months doesn't necessarily mean that it can't repeat it in the coming months. Sometimes, a stock at a higher price can be effectively cheaper than when it was in a lower range. For example, Beta Drugs was traded at the Rs 650–670 level in January 2022; at that time, the PE ratio was hovering around 50. After a few months, in May 2022, while the stock price was at the Rs 800–850 level, the PE ratio moderated to the 30–35 level due to earnings expansion. Moreover, future prospects for the company looked better after the FY2022 financial numbers and management conference calls. Thus, the stock at the 800–850 level turned out to be cheaper than it was when it was trading in the Rs 650–670 range.

'A stock price at Rs 800 can be effectively cheaper than it was at Rs 600.'

The stock price shouldn't be a consideration in the stock selection process. Investors frequently inquire about low-priced stocks thinking that they must be cheap. Don't have this misconception—the absolute value of the stock price has no correlation with valuation. It is not that stocks that are priced below Rs 10 can multiply your wealth quickly. In fact, most of these low-priced stocks are just trash. As of 2022, if you follow the historical stock price chart of Chemcrux Enterprises, you might think that back in 2017–18, the stock price was hovering at Rs 10–12 and this low level was why it generated more than forty times the returns. However, back in 2017–18, the stock price was actually in the Rs 30–36 range. Later, the company announced a 2:1 bonus, i.e., one share turned into three, and the stock price adjusted accordingly. In fact, in future, if the company opts for a 1:1 bonus or face-value split from Rs 10 to Rs 5 a share, then too the price will adjust accordingly and will look as if it was around Rs 5–6 during 2017–18. Similarly, the historical price chart of HDFC can suggest that the stock price was in the Rs 15–20 range back in 2001–02, but that is not the truth. The stock price was much higher, but because of the subsequent stock splits and bonus issues, it was adjusted in the historical chart.

Here is a list of well-known penny stocks (priced lower than Rs 10) and their price performance over the last year. I have considered only well-known ones in the following table. If you run a screener to get the price performance of all penny stocks, you will find a few hundred trashy companies.

Stock Name	Current Price Rs	1-year Change, Per cent	Market Cap, Rs Cr.
Suzlon Energy Ltd.	6.65	−13 per cent	6,509.60
Rattan India Power Ltd.	3.95	−47 per cent	2,121.20
IFCI Ltd.	9.85	−33 per cent	2,071.40
Jaiprakash Associates	7.45	−36 per cent	1,828.70
GTL Infrastructure Ltd	1.4	−59 per cent	1,767.30
South Indian Bank Ltd	7.95	−35 per cent	1,663.70
Reliance Communications	2.25	−40 per cent	622.2
Nagarjuna Fertilizers	8.95	−45 per cent	535.3
Unitech Ltd	1.65	−13 per cent	431.7
Future Consumer Ltd	1.9	−79 per cent	379.4
Parsvnath Developers	8.4	−53 per cent	365.6
Future Retail Ltd	6.35	−90 per cent	344.4

Fig. 7.2: List of well-known penny stocks with the last one-year price performance

Clearly, the chart shows that the current stock price has no correlation with the future prospects of a business. Chasing after low-priced stocks in the hope of multibagger returns can prove to be a very costly mistake.

> *'Never ever chase after low-priced penny stocks thinking that low price is one of the primary triggers for multibagger returns. In fact, the majority of low-priced stocks are actually wealth destroyers.'*

7.3 Don't Be a Forced Long-Term Investor

Mohit invested in a stock at Rs 100. His plan was to hold the stock for six to seven months and then exit at around 30–40 per cent profit. After six months, the stock price crashed by 40 per cent, with the company showing deteriorating business prospects. Mohit is now aware of the recent negative business development related to the company but is not willing to exit at a 40 per cent loss. Hoping that someday in the future he can recover the cost price, he has now converted into a 'long-term investor'. Initially, he was interested in mid-term swing trading, but adverse price movements forced him to become a long-term investor! How many of you have turned long-term investors, just like Mohit? I am sure there must be many. The majority of such investments end up bringing even more disappointment. The longer an investor holds an underperforming stock, the more his or her loss widens.

A similar mistake is often noticed in IPO investment. Making quick money in the listing day profit is an attractive short-term money-making proposition. Many investors apply for IPOs solely to benefit from the listing day profit.

However, if by any chance, things go in the opposite direction on the listing day, then many investors prefer to hold the shares and turn into forced long-term investors! Before entering into any trade, your intention must be clear. Similarly, before applying for any IPO, you must have a clear target in mind as to whether you are going to hold the shares for a longer run or participate just to gain from the short-term listing day profit. If your target is short-term listing day profit, then you must need to close the position on the listing day itself, irrespective of the profit or loss. If you keep holding the position just because of the listing day loss, hoping for gain in later days, then most likely the loss will widen further.

'Don't continue holding a consistent underperformer hoping that someday it will recover. In most such cases, loss widens further.'

7.4 Never Quit the Journey of Multibagger Investing

More than mastering the art of identifying multibaggers, you need to master the art of avoiding mistakes. And the biggest mistake one can make is quitting the journey of multibagger investing altogether. No matter what, you need to stay in the game to win, and if you can stay in the game long enough, then sooner or later, you will emerge as a winner.

Success in multibagger investing largely depends on how you react to losing instances. As you would have noticed in earlier chapters, multibagger returns mostly come from investing in the early stage of a company while the stock is 'less known', still in the small-cap/mid-cap phase and not widely covered by analysts, media, etc. Thus, the success ratio can be lower. If you limit your investments only to large-cap, established, well-known blue-chip companies for average returns, then your success rate can be pretty high. However, at a lower success rate, multibagger investing can yield much better returns in your overall portfolio. Have a look at the following chart:

	Blue-chip large-cap portfolio	Multibagger portfolio
Returns from Stock 1	Gain 10 per cent	Loss 40 per cent
Returns from Stock 2	Gain 15 per cent	Gain 200 per cent
Returns from Stock 3	Gain 20 per cent	Loss 50 per cent
Returns from Stock 4	Loss 15 per cent	Loss 60 per cent
Returns from Stock 5	Gain 18 per cent	Gain 160 per cent
Overall average return	**+11 per cent**	**+42 per cent**

As you can gather from the chart above, four out of five large-cap stocks generated positive returns—i.e., the success ratio was 80 per cent—and the overall returns were 11 per cent. However, in the multibagger portfolio, only two out of five stocks generated positive returns—i.e., the success rate was only 40 per cent—but the overall portfolio returns stand at 42 per cent. As it is clear now, multibagger investing entails a larger number of losing investments, so a large part of your success at it depends on how your mind responds to the losing instances.

'Success in multibagger investing largely depends on how you react in the losing instances.'

Having interacted with thousands of investors since 2013, I have noticed the following reactions when an investment goes sour:

1. Blaming one's own bad luck or lack of skill and feeling disappointed.
2. Blaming the adviser or the person who suggested the stock for investment.
3. Blaming the company management (founder, CEO, CFO, etc.)
4. Staying away from the stock market for a short period after multiple simultaneous losing instances, and sometimes permanently quitting the market.

You can pause for a moment and recall how you reacted the last time you made a loss on some investment. Most likely, you reacted in one of the five different ways described above. Fortunately, as I rely on my own research for my investments, 'blaming the adviser' does not apply to me, but I have been through all the other reactions. I am now going to share one of my own stories, having gained multiple insights into the investment journey.

Case study

It was April 2018. I had around eight years of active investing experience in the stock market under my belt and had already boosted my portfolio with multiple successful multibagger stocks. As my success rate with micro-cap/ SMEs/small-caps was pretty high, my entire portfolio was filled with SMEs and small-cap stocks. My confidence level was also high, as all those micro-cap stocks had multibagger potential. To my brutal surprise, within a few months beginning April 2018, my portfolio value dropped by one-third, with many of the stocks losing 30–80 per cent of their value! This was the status of my portfolio at the time:

	Nature of loss[*]	Time
Stock 1	Realized loss of 65 per cent	April 2018
Stock 2	Realized loss of 78 per cent	April–June 2018
Jhandewalas Foods	Realized loss of 50 per cent	April 2018
Sysco Industries	Realized loss of 85 per cent	April 2018
MRSS	Unrealized loss	May–June 2018
Focus Suites	Unrealized loss	May–June 2018
A few other stocks	Unrealized loss, 10–30 per cent	April–June 2018
Overall portfolio value declined by one-third within two months		April–June 2018

* Realized loss means the holdings were sold during the specified periods; unrealized loss refers to the loss on the stocks that were not yet sold in April–June 2018.

I was face to face with the first major setback in my investing career. That was the first time I was witnessing such a bloodbath in my portfolio. The worst part was, all of this happened very quickly, within the space of a couple of months. During that period, it was not just my portfolio that was dented; the entire mid-cap and small-cap segment in the Indian stock market suffered a huge setback. The frontline large-cap stocks were affected the least. There were many possible reasons for this setback:

1. Mutual fund reclassification by market regulator SEBI forced many mutual funds to dump their holdings in small-cap and micro-cap stocks.
2. Resignation of auditors from many firms due to tightening regulations.
3. Imposition of long-term capital gains tax, which spoilt investor sentiment.
4. Political uncertainty due to multiple assembly elections and the general election of the next year.

Due to the combination of varied reasons, the entire mid-cap and small-cap segment suffered, and so did my portfolio. What made matters worse is that my professional income also crashed as it came from my equity advisory services. At a time when the entire small-cap and mid-cap segment was bleeding badly and our recommended stocks were not performing well, retail investors were generally shying away from the service itself.

During this period, on 30 May 2018, one of my portfolio stocks, Chemcrux Enterprises, released its annual financial numbers for FY2018. Chemcrux was a micro-cap stock with a market cap of just Rs 15 crore at that time. The annual financial results were modest, but the interesting part about them lay in the management commentary, which said:

> *Chemcrux Enterprises would continue to drive volume-led growth in intermediate chemicals segment. Going forward, your Company foresees stronger customer relations, higher efficiencies and robust growth in demand of our intermediate chemicals in end user segment. We plan to take our next step forward to expand capacities and diversify by way of acquisitions in domestic market over the next 2 years. Our target is to achieve 30% growth in turnover for the FY 2018-19 with focus on overseas markets and exports. Your Company expects to deliver persistent growth year-on-year, combined with cost leadership and value-added product offerings, capacity expansion of captive plant, reduction in cost of manufacturing and diversification in new high value chemical products. Your company aims for digitisation of processes of purchase, sales, marketing and other operations over next year and gradual increase in manpower, facilities and office workspace.*
>
> (This commentary is available on the BSE India website under the Corporate Announcement segment for Chemcrux Enterprises under 'Press Release', dated 30 May 2018.)

A careful reading between the lines and closer scrutiny of the company financials made me realize that if everything goes well, then revenue growth for the next year, FY2019, would be much more than 30 per cent and could be as high as 50–70 per cent because the reported revenue for FY2018 had factored in two months of factory closure due to non-compliance of environmental norms. The total reported revenue for FY2018 was Rs 31 crore, which was actually the operational revenue for ten months. Extrapolating from these figures, the monthly revenue run rate was around Rs 3.1 crore and the yearly run rate would have been Rs 37–38 crore for FY2018 under normal circumstances. Applying the production growth rate of 30 per cent on Rs 38 crore, my FY2019 revenue estimation was over Rs 50 crore. Further, the company press release of 30 May 2018 had phrases like 'reduction in cost of manufacturing', 'diversification in high value chemical products', 'digitisation of processes', 'increase in office space', etc. My intuition told me that if all these factors came together, then the profit margin would experience a significant jump. Accordingly, I estimated the revenue for FY2019 at Rs 50–52 crore, with a net profit of Rs 7–8 crore, against the FY2018 revenue of Rs 31 crore and profit of Rs 2.36 crore. My eyes almost popped out as I saw the potential for a threefold jump in EPS and, in keeping with that, a potential stock price jump of 200 per cent in one to two years! Not only that, there was a high probability for PE ratio expansion. The sentiment towards the micro-cap SME segment was very weak during May–June 2018. Many micro-cap stocks were crashing by 40–60 per cent in those two or three months. I guessed that if the sentiment improved by 2019, then PE re-rating would further feed gains in the stock price of Chemcrux. Overall, there was a high probability of a 200+ per cent jump (more than threefold return) in the stock price and one should buy the stock in truckloads.

However, my state of mind was completely shaken at the same time due to the recent huge loss from similar micro-cap SME stocks. The wound was still fresh. During the same period of May–June 2018, I had actually booked a huge loss on four stocks—of 65 per cent, 78 per cent, 50 per cent and 85 per cent. The remaining micro-cap stocks in my portfolio at that time were also losing value every day and I was staring at a 20–50 per cent unrealized loss on those stocks. Within those two months, the sentiment towards micro-cap and small-cap stocks had changed so drastically that investors were shying away from the entire segment.

My portfolio value was already lost by one-third and was still bleeding. It is only if you have suffered such a huge loss in a short period of one or two months and also found the entire market bleeding at the same time that you can fathom how I must have felt at the time. It cannot be described in words; you have to experience it to know what it is like. If you were an active investor during 2000–02, 2008–09, 2013 or 2018 (in small-caps and mid-caps), then you might empathize with me. Such a blow, especially after your investments have been done after in-depth analysis, can hit your confidence and leave you with little courage to invest in truckloads in another similar SME stock, Chemcrux Enterprises. On one hand, my analysis was showing a more-than-three-times-returns possibility and on another hand, I had suffered a huge setback relying on my similar analysis! Most importantly, If I was proven wrong again in Chemcrux, then whatever I had earned in the past eight years would have all been gone!

Reason for buying Chemcrux in truckloads	Reasons for NOT investing in Chemcrux
My analysis was showing a more-than-three-times-returns potential from this low-volume SME stock.	Just suffered huge realized loss from similar micro-cap SME stocks.
	Every day, unrealized loss in portfolio was increasing as micro-cap and small-cap stocks were tanking.
	The entire segment of micro-cap, small-cap and mid-cap was bleeding profusely and investors were shying away, shifting to large-caps.
	Being a low-volume illiquid stock, a single negative development (like factory closure) could result in a quick downfall and back-to-back lower circuit in the stock price leaving no option to exit at minimal loss.
	If Chemcrux went wrong, then whatever I had earned in the past eight years would have all been gone.

It was a tough dilemma; on one hand, plenty of reasons to avoid the stock and on another hand, the possibility of threefold returns. I had only two options:

1. Irrespective of the loss, keep faith in my own analysis and conviction, and back myself in tough times to stage a stronger comeback.

2. Accepting the defeat in micro-cap investing and playing safe, limiting investment only to the large-cap segment, or even worse, quitting the stock market altogether.

I chose the first option. Despite the fact that I couldn't afford another setback, I went ahead buying truckloads of the stock, Chemcrux Enterprises, and the rest is history.

Here is the summarized timeline of my investment:

March–April 2017 (market capitalization Rs 15–16 crore): This is the time I first invested in Chemcrux just after it hit the market with its IPO. The stock price didn't move anywhere for the next one and a half years. One of the primary negative developments during the period was a factory shutdown due to non-compliance of some environmental norms.

June 2018 (market capitalization Rs 15–16 crore): The biggest trigger for increasing my investment in the company came in the form of the company press release dated 30 May 2018. I bought more shares in the company despite all the adversities discussed earlier and zero returns from the stock over the last year. The historical shareholding pattern available on the BSE website would reveal my huge increase in investment.

August–September 2018 (market capitalization Rs 15–16 crore): Unfortunately, the stock price remained subdued till September 2018, even after such encouraging management commentary. Due to negative sentiment, micro-cap stocks were not reacting to any positive development, but any negative development puts immense pressure on the price. Despite that, I increased my investment in Chemcrux once again in August 2018, and by then, the stock was the largest holding in my portfolio.

November 2018–June 2020: In 2019, the stock price doubled from the 2018 level. But then again, after the emergence of COVID-19 in early 2020, the stock price went nowhere till mid-2020, although in between, the earnings registered an almost fivefold jump.

2021 onwards: After a long wait of three years, finally, the sentiment towards the micro-cap segment improved. Expansion in earnings (EPS) was present in all the past four to five years and in 2021, improved sentiment paved the way for PE ratio expansion. As a result, at the time of writing this book, the stock price is showing more than forty times the returns from my initial investment!

Thus, a careful study reveals that my investment rationale was spot on since 2017, but the reward was missing over three to four years. Had I quit during adversities in 2018, the story would have been completely different. Instead of quitting micro-cap investment, I continued my learning quest with eyes and ears open, and continued backing the conviction that eventually helped me discover several other multibagger picks—Lancer Container, Sirca Paints, Gujarat Themis Biosyn, Prevest Denpro, SKP Bearings, Bombay Metrics Supply Chain and many others.

'No matter what, never quit the stock market. Sooner or later, you will face setbacks. Your reaction during adverse times decides success in multibagger investment.'

7.5 The Importance of Luck in Getting Multibagger Returns

Yes, luck matters, not only in the stock market but also in every other aspect of our lives. Whether it is a cricket match, an election or a corporate activity, luck plays an important role in determining the outcome. However, what I have observed is that luck favours the most deserving candidate. Remember the India vs Bangladesh cricket match in the Nidahas Trophy final in March 2018, where Dinesh Karthik alone rescued India from a losing position? You may recall another India vs Bangladesh cricket match in the 2016 T20 World Cup tournament, where the famous last ball stumping of M.S. Dhoni stunned everyone. I am referring to cricket because that is the most-viewed sport in India. You can watch the highlights of the matches on YouTube. Anyone can conclude that on both occasions, India was just lucky to win the game. However, in my view, luck favoured India only because the Indian players were more skilful and handled the pressure well compared with their Bangladeshi counterparts.

A person can win Rs 1 crore in the lottery simply because of luck, but without skill, he can't maintain that Rs 1 crore to remain wealthy. However, a deserving person will turn that Rs 1 crore into Rs 10 crore and then again turn that Rs 10 crore into Rs 100 crore. If you offer Rs 10 crore to Mukesh Ambani, he can easily convert that to Rs 1000 crore. The skill of multiplying money that Mukesh Ambani and other billionaire businesspeople possess is lacking in common people and that's why, when it comes to money, luck favours Mukesh Ambani. Many of you might keep complaining that all the wealthy people on the planet are just born lucky, but careful observation reveals that, without skills, the same person can't remain wealthy. There are enough examples of billionaires ending up bankrupt. So, luck always favours the most deserving candidate.

In investing as well, luck favours the deserving candidate most. I was not the only one who invested in Lancer Container, Sirca Paints, Chemcrux Enterprises, KP Energy and others back in 2017–18; there were hundreds of other investors who took positions in one or the other stocks during the same period, but the end result of investment differs from person to person. A few investors ended up with a modest profit and a few others were even at a loss in the overall portfolio. My overall portfolio value jumped multifold because I kept on increasing investment where the earning expansion possibility was bright and weeding out underperformers where the earning expansion possibility was non-existent. My luck favoured me in 2021–22 only after the persistence of four long years since 2017.

Thus, one should not worry about the contribution of luck in investing. You need to remember that luck eventually finds the most deserving candidate. You just need to stay in the game and continue travelling in the right direction. Sooner or later, luck will favour you for sure.

Frequently Asked Questions

Q1 How has your portfolio strategy evolved over the years?

When I started my investment journey, I was still a teenager. I had no financial liabilities and there was no compulsion on me to earn, and that helped a lot. I was free to experiment with the little capital I had. And I had more than enough time for learning. From 2010 to 2016, my focus was solely on low-volume small-cap stocks that had multibagger potential. However, during the 2018 liquidity crunch, I realized that having 100 per cent of your portfolio consisting of low-volume stocks is not a good idea when you have financial commitments towards family or have business expenses to make. So, from 2018–19, I began to maintain two different segments in my portfolio:

1. **High-volume stocks**: These were mostly mid-cap and large-cap stocks. This part of my portfolio is for any kind of emergency cash withdrawal. Although

I maintain enough emergency funds outside my equity investments, still, should any unfortunate event arise, this portion of my portfolio can be liquidated easily.

2. **Low-volume stocks**: This segment consists of micro-cap and small-cap stocks that have multibagger returns potential. These are illiquid stocks, so they are difficult to exit at any particular point in time. The plan is to never make any forced withdrawals from this segment. This part is only for aggressive portfolio expansion.

Depending on the situation, I mostly maintain a 50:50 or 60:40 allocation ratio of low-volume and high-volume stocks in my portfolio and the details are available on my website.

Q2 Can I invest in any of the stocks mentioned in the book? Will you notify me when you exit from any of your investments described in the book?

The book is for educational purposes. Stocks mentioned in the book are used to illustrate theoretical concepts. Investing in any such stock carries a huge amount of risk because future prospects can change by the time you read the book. It is not feasible to announce my exit decision to all readers before selling a stock. Remember, more than buying a stock, it is the holding period that determines multibagger returns. Today, if I am positive on any stock, it doesn't necessarily mean I will remain positive on it tomorrow also. Any single-day event can alter the prospects of a business, making me change my decision. Don't expect replies to emails or social media messages asking for views on any particular stock because, after a few days, while my views can change, it would be impossible to trace your contact and communicate again. Instead, focus on learning the ropes. On our website, www.prasenjitpaul.com, you will find services that can help you become self-reliant in multibagger hunting.

Q3 I am a complete beginner, just acquainted with the stock market. Kindly guide me on how I should navigate properly in multibagger investing.

First remember, slow and steady wins the race. Never be in a hurry in the wealth creation journey. Every quick money-making opportunity is actually a money-losing opportunity. Whoever lost a huge sum in the stock market did so only because of the urge to make money quickly. Obviously, multibagger investing can yield ten to twelve times the returns in the portfolio over a period of a few years, but to accomplish that, you need years-long preparation. You can't expect multifold returns in your initial years.

So, keep your expectation low and invest more time in acquiring knowledge. It is absolutely fine if you seek any external stock advice or recommendation. However, don't invest blindly, no matter where the stock recommendation is coming from. Prepare an elaborate checklist with the help of this book and educational content available on our website, and before investing, make sure you fill up the entire checklist. The investment rationale or why you are investing must be clear beforehand. Be prepared for the best-case and worst-case scenarios and deploy capital accordingly. After the investment, make sure you track all company-specific updates, business announcements and financial results to stay up-to-date. Don't get bothered about daily price movement. However, if any significant price movement coincides with positive or negative developments, then it's time to be alert. Finally, hold the stock as long as the earning and PE expansion possibility is present and exit from the stock when the earning and PE expansion probability diminishes. Repeat the process multiple times over a period of a few years, and you will reach your goal.

Q4 What are the other books written by you?

My first book, *How to Avoid Loss and Earn Consistently in the Stock Market*, was an instant hit. Since its publication in 2015 until 2022, more than 2 lakh copies have been sold. Most of the readers find the book an easy-to-read and practical guide to navigating the investment journey properly. The book has also been translated into Hindi, Marathi, Tamil and Gujarati; a few translations in regional languages are in the pipeline.

This is my second book after a gap of many years. Writing a book requires months-long concentration and a distraction-free mind over a prolonged period, which is always challenging in our fast-paced lifestyle. Nevertheless, I will surely write more books in the future. If you wish to receive notifications about my upcoming books or seminars/webinars, you can register your email at www.prasenjitpaul.com or join our free Telegram channel t.me/PrasenjitPaulVerified.

Similar to many other public figures, many fake Telegram channels are using my picture and name to dupe investors. In my original channel, you will find a profile picture with the statement, 'I never give tips on Crypto, Futures and Options. Never offer return guarantee.' If anywhere on the Internet, someone using my name and picture offers any sort of guaranteed returns or quick money-making scheme or suggestion on cryptocurrencies or intraday or futures and options, then be sure that's not me.

Q5 You mostly focus on fundamental analysis for spotting multibagger stocks. Don't you think technical analysis plays an important role as well?

Technical analysis proves beneficial in high-volume, widely-traded stocks. For multibaggers, you need to focus on micro-cap or small-cap stocks that are still in the early stage of the business life cycle with huge growth potential ahead. Trading volume is minimal in micro-cap and small-cap stocks. In fact, many micro-cap stocks are not even traded daily! Technical analysis stands on the trading volume and price movement. Thus, in the absence of sufficient trading volume, technical analysis becomes redundant. This is the reason you will find many micro-cap stocks often move in the upper circuit or lower circuit, ignoring support/resistance level. For large-cap and mid-cap widely-traded, high-volume stocks, technical analysis is useful, but the same is not the case with low-volume micro-cap and small-cap stocks.

Q6 What would be your final piece of advice before venturing into multibagger hunting?

Remember, success in a multibagger journey depends on how long you can stay in the game without being injured badly. Here, injury refers to wiping out capital. Remember, if you lose 50 per cent of your capital, then just for capital recovery, it requires 100 per cent returns! If your Rs 1 lakh investment turns to Rs 50,000, then just to bring it back to Rs 1 lakh would require 100 per cent returns on Rs 50,000. Similarly, if you lose 60 per cent of your capital, then just for capital recovery it requires 150 per cent returns. The higher the loss, the more difficult it would become to stay in the game. Generally, after a 50–60 per cent loss in micro-cap investing, most investors prefer to opt out and search for safe bets in large-cap names, which in turn diminishes the chances of ten to fifty times the returns that a micro-cap portfolio offers. To avoid major capital loss while hunting for multibaggers in the small-cap and micro-cap space, if any of the following parameters holds true, avoid the stock:

1. Cyclical business.
2. Business with no pricing power; can't pass on input price hikes to end customer.
3. Business with no competitive advantage or moat.
4. Business with absolutely zero entry barriers. Anyone with nominal capital can start the same business.
5. Difficult-to-understand business.
6. Historical (last five or ten years) net profit margin shows a highly volatile trend.
7. Company showing inflated profits just before IPO.
8. Debt-to-equity ratio is more than 1.
9. Overall debt increasing significantly every year over the last three years.
10. ROE and ROCE are both less than 12 per cent.
11. Both ROE and ROCE are decreasing every year for the last three years.
12. Promoter holding less than 50 per cent.

13.   Promoter group selling their stake.
14.   Promoters have pledged part of their shareholding.
15.   Cash flow from operations (CFO) is negative every year for the last three years.
16.   Too much social media hype and many market participants suggesting investment in that particular stock.
17.   You are getting free tips on the stock from unknown sources via SMS, email or on Telegram/WhatsApp.

Remember, the above list is valid only for micro-cap and small-cap investing; it does not apply to large-cap and mid-cap stocks. Further, a stock can still generate positive returns if any of the above parameters hold true. All I mean to say is, if rigorously followed, the above 'List to Avoid' can help you save a major capital loss in your multibagger journey. Without a major capital loss, if you can stick to an active micro-cap investing journey over a period of ten to twenty years, then, irrespective of initial capital, you are bound to earn multiple crores!

Wishing you wealth and prosperity from the multibagger journey!

Acknowledgements

This book has been my dream project for many years. I have been fortunate enough to survive and prosper in equity investing, which has turned my dream of writing a book into a reality.

First, I would like to thank God, the Almighty, for countless blessings and opportunities. Next, I would like to express my gratitude to my parents, wife and sister for their unconditional support.

Many thanks to Abhijeet Anand, Anupam Maity and Shouvik Ghosh, my associates at Paul Asset. They never turned me down, whatever I asked for. They have made an immense contribution to my successful career.

I would also like to thank a few lakhs of retail investors who opted for our various services or subscribed to our social channels like YouTube, Telegram, Instagram, Facebook, etc. They helped me realize their difficulties in equity investing. This book is an attempt to assist them in earning big from the stock market.

A big thank you to the Penguin publication team, Manish and Ralph, for encouraging me and turning this book into a reality. It has been many years of hard work and team efforts, which have finally taken shape.

Last but not least, special thanks to Microsoft, Google and Adobe for the numerous utility tools that helped me draft and prepare the manuscript of this book!